ב"ה

Bustenai

Adapted by
Eva Jacobson Hartheimer

From the text of
Dr. Marcus Lehman

Illustrated by
Zalman Kleinman

Published and Copyrighted by
MERKOS L'INYONEI CHINUCH
770 EASTERN PARKWAY, BROOKLYN, NEW YORK 11213
5773 / 2012

BUSTENAI

Revised Edition Copyright © 1982
Second Printing 1994
Third Printing 2012

by
Merkos L'Inyonei Chinuch
770 Eastern Parkway / Brooklyn, New York 11213
(718) 774-4000 / FAX (718) 774-2718
editor@kehot.com

Order Department:
291 Kingston Avenue / Brooklyn, New York 11213
(718) 778-0226 / FAX (718) 778-4148
www.kehot.com

All rights reserved.

The Merkos & Kehot logos are trademarks of Merkos L'Inyonei Chinuch.

ISBN: 978-0-8266-0035-6
ISBN: 978-0-8266-0033-2 (set)

Printed in China

PREFACE

This expanded adaptation of the novel Bustenai as well as the first edition, is for the most part, adapted from the text of Dr. Marcus Lehman (1831-1890), noted author of the 19th century, which first appeared in German. In addition, a Hebrew version of the German text, by Shmuel Yosef Pinn, published in Vilna in 1872, that was provided by the library of the Lubavitcher Rebbe שליט"א, was an invaluable aid in the preparation of this volume.

Eva Jacobson Hartheimer
Lag B'omer, 5742
May 11, 1982
New York, N.Y.

BUSTENAI

Chapter One

y the waters of Babylon, in the year 4,360 (600 C.E.), sounds of gladness and jubilation rang out wherever Jews dwelt. The harps were taken down from the willows, and the Jews rejoiced and sang the songs of their beloved Zion.

Mar Huna, son of Rabbi Chanina, the Resh Galuta or Leader-in-Exile, and Yaleta, the daughter of the renowned scholar, Rabbi Chafni, were to be wed.

The Resh Galuta, Mar Chanina, was a scion of the royal house of David. This line had endured, unbroken, despite defeat and dispersion by its conquerors, the enemies of the Jews. The marriage would preserve the lineage of this dynasty until the day when all Jews scattered in exile would return to the promised land, the land of Israel.

The hope and elation sparked by the news of the wedding were in sharp contrast to the fear and gloom that hung over the Jews of Babylon. Gloom and anxiety, however, were swept aside as preparations for the wedding were begun.

Tents of richly-colored silks and tapestries,

resting on posts of ornately carved wood, were mounted on the banks of the Euphrates in Mechuza, where the wedding was to take place. From near and far, Jews flocked to celebrate the union of the families of scholars and of princes that held so much promise for the future of the Jewish people.

On the appointed day, multitudes lined the sun-parched roads leading to the wedding site. Shouts of welcome mingled with gasps of wonderment as the gold-bedecked carriage of Rabbi Chanina, flanked by an escort of fifty guards attired in gold-embroidered livery, emerged from the cloud of dust. In this carriage rode Mar Chanina, Rabbi Chafni, and his brothers.

"Peace unto you!" — the cry rose from thousands of voices.

"Long life to our Prince, Mar Chanina!"

Another carriage, adorned with gold and silver, flying silken banners, and escorted by richly-liveried attendants, came into view.

"Long life to Prince Mar Huna!" shouted the multitudes, for the bridegroom, accompanied by his brothers, sat in that carriage. To the music of a hundred musical instruments and the thunderous applause of the throngs, Mar Huna alit from the carriage.

In the distance, another carriage was seen approaching. Like the others preceding it, this coach dazzled the sight of all beholders with its gilt and silver ornamentations and its guard of golden-plumed horsemen. The heavily-veiled Yaleta, her mother, and Mar Huna's sister rode in this carriage.

"Long life to the pure Yaleta, Mother of the tribe of Judah! Princess of the house of David!" The voices were raised in exultant welcome.

Many more coaches arrived bearing relatives and friends. Mari bar Mar, head of the great Torah academy at Pombedethah, was to perform the wedding ceremony.

At last, the bride and groom stood side by side under the outspread Chupah. Rabbi Mari bar Mar, with wine goblet in his hand, chanted the initial blessings of the marriage ceremony. When Mar Huna slipped the wedding ring on the finger of his bride, the crowd could no longer contain its enthusiasm. Deafening roars and applause broke forth from the bystanders. It seemed that the throng would cheer forever, had it not finally heeded the call for silence, so that the Ktubah (Marriage Contract) could be read and the ceremony concluded with the reciting of the Seven Blessings.

Afterwards, the tables were laid for the sumptuous wedding feast. What unbridled merriment and what boundless rejoicing attended that feast! The joyous sounds of song and dance overflowed the riverbanks and spread throughout Mechuza.

A halt in the festivities was requested, and, in the tradition of scholarly families, the groom, Mar Huna, delivered a discourse worthy of his father-in-law, the eminent Rabbi Chafni. All listened in rapt attention, but none as carefully as the parents of the birde and groom. Rabbi Chanina glowed with pride, and Rabbi Chafni beamed with happiness as Mar Huna spoke.

As the celebrations drew to a close, Mar Huna raised his goblet and proclaimed:

"Dear friends, I do not presume that you have come here today in my honor; I know that you are here to honor my father, my ancestors, and the House of David. Alas, the crown now lies in the dust, and the Holy Temple is destroyed. Again and again we have suffered persecution at the hands of our enemies. How long shall G-d let it continue? How long shall the House of David remain in exile?"

"Today I have taken the pious Yaleta for my wife. Let it be G-d's will that from this union there shall emerge a redeemer of our people who, in the near future, may lead us back to our Holy Land!"

A thunderous roar of assent rose from the entire assemblage:

"May it be G-d's will! Oh may it be G-d's will!"

Chapter Two

t the time of this wedding, King Kuzroi II sat on the throne of Persia. Before his succession to the throne, he had led a turbulent life. His father, King Hermiz IV, jealous of the popularity enjoyed by his general Bahram, ousted him from office. In retaliation, Bahram, with the support of the army, wrested the Persian crown from the king. Hermiz was imprisoned; his eyes were gouged out, and later he was put to death.

Kuzroi, the crown prince, escaped to Rome where he enlisted the aid of Emperor Moritsius. Prince Kuzroi gratefully accepted the army that was offered to him. Aided by the Persian nobles from the border dominions, Kuzroi entered Ktesipon, the Persian stronghold, and forced Bahram to flee. Kuzroi's enemies, among whom he counted the Jews, who had hailed Bahram's revolt as a deliverance from the tyrannical Hermiz, were bitterly persecuted.

Kuzroi also set about increasing the wealth of the crown at the expense of his enemies. Before long, he had erected many magnificent palaces and had accumulated many treasures and great riches. All this made him realize how great was the debt that he owed to the Roman emperor Moritsius.

One day a note was brought to Kuzroi stating that Theophenus, the son of Emperor Moritsius, was asking for an audience with the king. Kuzroi was surprised that the son of the Roman emperor should come unescorted, and he had him brought in immediately. Theophenus entered, and the tidings that he brought set the court into turmoil. Cries of lamentation and dismay filled the royal chamber.

"The Emperor Moritsius," the boy announced, "has been assassinated. But," he continued bravely, "I have not come here for sympathy. I have come here to ask you to aid me as my father once assisted you in your time of need, and to avenge the death of my father and brothers, and the disgrace of my mother and sisters."

Grieved by the ignoble death of his former benefactor, Kuzroi readily assented. "But tell me, " he said, "how did this treacherous deed come to pass?"

"My father," Theophenus began, "had aroused the wrath of the Roman soldiery by prohibiting their disorderly behavior. They rebelled and proclaimed their chief, Pokas, emperor. My father tried to flee from the barbarians with his family, but I was the only one who escaped death. Now Pokas rules with utter brutality. Throughout the empire, many people are slaughtered every day, and even more are forced to undergo the cruel tortures that these savages have devised. I appeal to you, for the sake of my father and his family who were so viciously murdered, to punish these beasts, and restore the throne to its rightful heir."

The king warmly embraced the young prince and promised that he would root out the vandals responsible for the death of the noble Moritsius. He provided him with a palace and other needs befitting an emperor's son. When a messegner, sent by Pokas, came to inform the king that Rome now had a new emperor, he was immediately imprisoned. King Kuzroi was preparing for war.

He summoned all the princes of the kingdom, including Mar Chanina and his son Huna, to inform them of the political situation. When the princes heard Theophenus's report, they pledged their loyalty and support to the king. War it was; war against anarchy and insurgence. A plan of action was quickly drawn up. Mesopotamia was to be attacked first, then the states bordering on Persia. Judea would be next. If these campaigns were successful, Constantinople and the territories beyond it that were under Roman rule would be invaded. The princes were ordered to mobilize their troops.

"Chanina," the king said at length, "weren't your ancestors the kings of the Holy Land?"

"Yes," he answered. "Your servant is a descendant of the House of David."

"If we are victorious," the king continued, "it is possible that your dynasty may once more rule over this land. Supply me with twenty thousand troops, and I will appoint either you or your son — as you wish — governor of the province of Judea. There you will be able to assemble Jews from all the corners of the earth and rebuild your Holy Temple."

"I have too many years behind me," Chanina said, "to lead an army into the fray. My son Huna will take command; you will find his troops in the forefront of the battle.."

"G-d speed your victory," Huna joined in. "Thirty thousand brave youths shall be at your command and, with G-d's help, they will bring you triumph and fame."

Chapter Three

hroughout Persia the impending war gave rise to feverish activity. In every province troops were assembled and sent to join the main Persian forces. The glittering hope of a new Jewish kingdom in the Holy Land brought the Jews from the most distant districts to the city of Mechuza. Inspired by this vision, they left their families and brought their courage and strength to the army of Huna. Thirty thousand Jewish warriors stood under arms; Huna's promise to the king was fulfilled. Then they marched to join the main body of the Persian army.

City after city and state after state fell to the advancing Persian legions. They crossed the Euphrates and approached the walls of Antioch, the city that held so many painful memories for the Jews. With the cry, "The fall of Antioch means the rise of Jerusalem," Huna's army flung itself against the city's walls with wondrous bravery. Soon the city was in Persian hands, and to the Jews went the credit for its conquest.

Steadily, the Persian armies pressed forward. Damascus and Kisrun fell, and several days later the vanguard of the Persian army crossed the border of the Holy Land and entered Galil. Mar Huna and his men were at the head of the troops. When their feet touched the sacred earth, they prostrated themselves and kissed it. Then, remembering the glory of the land that had passed with the destruction of the Temple, they raised their voices in bitter lament and tore their clothes in mourning.

The news of Mar Huna's arrival spread throughout the country, and Jews from all parts of the Holy Land came to join in the march to capture the city of Jerusalem. The defenders could not long withstand the assault of the Persian catapults that shattered their walls, and soon the invaders were within the city. The Persians celebrated their victory by burning the city and massacring and pillaging its Roman inhabitants; the Jews made their way to the the Western Wall, all that was left standing of the Temple. There, with prayers and tears, they mourned the blight and decay that had ravaged their holiest treasure.

The end of the war came more quickly than anticipated, for it was speeded by the overthrow of Pokas. Subsequently, it was discovered that the young man who claimed to be the son of the Emperor Moritsius was really no more than one of his liberated slaves.

Mar Huna now reminded the king of his promise to permit the establishment of a Jewish state. To his great surprise and dismay, he received a scathing reply:

"Do you dare to demand this of me?" the king stormed. "I know that if I name you Prince of Judea, your lust for power will lead you to defy my authority. You will join forces with the Roman emperor and set up an independent state!"

"But have I not been a loyal servant?" Mar Huna asked. "Have not my troops led your men into battle more than twenty times?"

"Your troops! They are my troops as are all the other Persian forces. Already you think that you are king of the Jews because you are a descendant of David. If I hear you say one word more on the subject, you will pay for it with your head!"

With a heart full of bitterness and anger, Mar Huna left the king's palace.

The news of the king's betrayal on his promise to the Jews was received with grief and distress. Once again the Jews had been beguiled into shedding their blood for promises that were not kept. Once again they had willingly sacrificed their lives for their beloved land, only to discover that they were the victims of a cruel jest. As for Kuzroi, all the victories that G-d granted him for the sake of the Jews, he credited to himself.

The disappointment of the Jews gave rise to agitation and defiance. They were still twenty-six thousand strong; they urged Huna to cease his useless lamentation and in the tradition of David lead them into war against the Persian king. Only one voice was raised in dissent. Benjamin, the leader of the Eretz Israel warriors, approached Mar Huna and advised him against taking such a course.

"The time is not ripe," he said, "for us to re-establish our kingdom. Once before, under the Emperor Julian, the Jews were offered the opportunity to rebuild their Temple, but because the time had not yet come, they did not succeed. I shall now tell you what the great Rabbi Joshua told them at that time. 'Let us be satisfied and thank G-d that we are still alive. Let the king's treachery be a sign that it is still too early to rely upon the promises of a heathen. Let us return to our wives and children, to our parents and friends who are waiting for us. The Maccabees fought to defend their religion; it was their sacred duty to fight against overwhelming odds. But our reasons are different. We have no right to match ourselves against an army of such awesome strength."

This counsel, however, was not heeded by the rest.

"Victory or death!" was their reply, and they prepared for battle.

The rebellion came to a speedy end. The king's army was immediately sent to suppress the revolt. Although the outnumbered Jews put up a courageous and bloody fight, they were quickly surrounded and faced certain annihilation.

Suddenly the Persians ceased their slaughter, and an emissary from the king approached the Jewish camp. The king, he informed them, had not forgotten the part that they had played in the last campaign. He was willing to permit them all to return to their homes in peace if they would hand over Mar Huna as a captive. If they refused, not only they, but their families at home, would be slain without mercy.

Not one of the Jews entertained, even for one moment, the thought of surrendering Mar Huna to the enemy. Mar Huna himself arose and approached the emissary.

"Did the king say whether he wanted me killed, or brought prisoner?" he asked.

"Dead or alive," was the answer.

"Then tell your king that my death shall lie on his head like a curse. The day will come when he will be betrayed as he betrayed those who were faithful to him, and he will die a horrible death!" And turning to his followers, Huna continued: "And you, my brethren, may your lives be happy. Too early I attempted to restore the throne of David; now I must leave you. Bring my greetings to my aged father, my mother and sisters, and to my beloved wife Yaleta. The child that she will bear will never know its father. Console them for me. And now, G-d of the Universe, I give you back my soul. Forgive my sin of taking my own life, for it is to save the lives of my brethren. Hear O Israel! The L-rd is our G-d, The L-rd is One!" With the echoes of his last words ringing through the air, he plunged his sword into his heart.

Chapter Four

naware of both the Jewish revolt and of the death of Mar Huna, the Jews in the city of Mechuza rejoiced over the Persian victories. Chanina received a dispatch from the king inviting him with his entire family to the capital for the celebration of his triumphs. Accompanied by fifty footmen and twelve riders, the unsuspecting Chanina sat alone in his gilded carriage, followed by a procession of other carriages in which rode all the descendants of the House of David with their families. Only Yaleta, who was expecting a child, remained at home. When they arrived they were immediately ushered into the presence of the king. There Chanina prostrated himself and thanked the king for his promise to re-establish the crown of the House of David.

"I see," said the king after an ominous silence, "that as long as the House of David remains in existence, the Jews will never be loyal subjects of the king. Even now they give their G-d credit for my victories. Your son Huna died a traitor, and the same fate awaits your entire family!"

At a signal from the king, several of his guards

bore down on the Jewish royal family. Over one hundred of the descendants of David fell that day at the feet of the Persian king. To insure the success of his plan, the king sent a messenger to kill Yaleta, for he was determined to completely annihilate the House of David; only then would his mind be at ease. But the hand of G-d saved Yaleta from the fate that had overtaken Chanina and his family. Benjamin, the leader of the Eretz Israel army, realizing that Mar Huna's death meant that the entire family was in danger, had sped to Mechuza to urge them to escape. But it was too late; Chanina and the others were already on their way to the king's palace.

Benjamin did not dare tell Yaleta, in her condition, of the death of her husband and the probable fate of the entire family. Without saying more than that he was a comrade-in-arms of Huna, he told Yaleta that she must escape from the city without delay.

Instinctively she felt she could believe the man's words and trust him. She quickly had a carriage prepared in which she, Benjamin, and one of her loyal servants, would make the trip to the house of Yaleta's father in Sura.

As soon as they arrived at Rabbi Chafni's house, Benjamin explained the situation to him. Rabbi Chafni did not doubt the man's words and, losing no time, he dressed Yaleta in the tattered clothing of an impoverished woman and sent her to live with a poor family in little town far from Sura.

Soon Kuzroi's agents, having discovered that Yaleta had fled from Mechuza, descended upon Rabbi Chafni's house in search of her. When they could not find Yaleta, they imprisoned Rabbi Chafni and subjected him to unspeakable torture to compel him to reveal his daughter's hiding place. Despite the pain that wracked his limbs, Rabbi Chafni's lips remained sealed.

Yaleta's disappearance was the only thing that marred Kuzroi's happiness. The king now considered himself the greatest ruler that ever lived. Poets and writers were commanded to praise him for his deeds, which supposedly surpassed those of his predecessors. He had magnificent palaces built, and his treasury was full of the loot of conquered countries. This contentment, however, did not last. One morning the king awoke with a mysterious wound in his forehead from which blood gushed forth in a scarlet stream.

How he had received the wound, the king did not know. All he remembered was that in his dream he had seen a figure strike his head with an axe. When he had been bandaged by the court physician, he called upon his wizards to interpret his terrifying dream. Like Nebuchadnezzar, Kuzroi threatened them with death if they would not tell him the meaning of the dream, but still they could not offer any explanation.

The mysterious dream haunted the king constantly. The vision he saw in his dream was always before his eyes, and he soon fell into a state of profound melancholy.

When the news of the king's distress reached the prison, Rabbi Chafni offered to go to the palace and interpret the dream. Rabbi Chafni insisted on appearing before the king in the tattered, blood-stained clothing he wore in his prison cell. He hoped that this sight would remind Kuzroi of the innocent blood he had shed and would finally arouse his conscience. Thus, Kuzroi might be lead to the path of repentance through which he would be cured of his affliction.

The king was infuriated by Rabbi Chafni's appearance.

"What!" he screamed. "Do you dare come to the king like this?"

"It is you who garbed me thus," Chafni answered quietly.

"Is that the way you dare to speak to the sovereign of the world! I will have you killed for that!"

"Kill me if you wish; the misery that I have experienced through your tyranny has not made living worthwhile. But then you will never learn the secret of your dream, and you will grow insane with anguish."

The king shuddered, then said more amiably:

"Do you mean to say that you know my dream and its meaning?"

"Indeed I do," Rabbi Chafni replied. "It was on the first night of the new moon." He continued, "You

were strolling along the banks of the Euphrates in a fertile region."

"That's right! Now I remember! I was at my summer palace on the river bank. It was dawn, and I was admiring the beauty of my surroundings in the light of the rising sun. My heart was filled with indescribable joy, and I cried out: 'What a beautiful world! And it is mine, all mine!' But wait; the picture fades. What did I do next?"

"You entered a beautiful garden that surpassed in beauty and in color anything that had ever been created."

"Yes, I remember now. I was overwhelmed by the splendor of the different trees and flowers in the garden. The fragrance that filled my nostrils and the sight of the ripe, luscious fruit made me think I was in the garden of Eden. I asked the servant at the gate the name of the owner, but I do not recall the answer. In fact I can remember nothing further."

"You became violently angry and cried out: 'Who dares to possess a garden in my kingdom that surpasses the finest that I own!' You seized an axe and began to chop down the rows of stately trees with the fury of a maniac. All that remained after you had given vent to your insanity was one slender sapling that had just been planted and had not yet begun to sprout. Even this you were about to destroy, when suddenly . . . ."

"When suddenly a patriarchal old man appeared before my eyes. He shouted at me in anger, and he struck me on the forehead with the axe that he wrested out of my hand. He threatened to kill me for destroying his wonderful garden, and I threw myself at his feet and pleaded for my life. I offered him the best gardens in my kingdom, but he spurned the exchange. His trees, he declared, were superior to any that I could give him, and their fruit could nowhere else be found. I pleaded with him and swore that if he would spare me, I would care for the last remaining sapling, water it, and protect it until it grew to be a strong tree. Then, from the seeds of that tree, he would be able to plant his garden once more . . . ."

"And the owner of the garden, moved by your tears, pleas, and solemn pledge, spared your life. He warned you, however, that if as much as one twig of the tree should be harmed, your life would be forfeited."

The king's face lit up, as the entire dream was now revealed to him. Then, recalling the blow he had received in his dream, the smile vanished from his face, and he said:

"On that very morning that I awoke and found the wound in my head. I knew that I had had a terrible dream, but until you came to my assistance, I could hardly recall a fragment of it. Perhaps you also know the interpretation of my strange dream?"

"That I do. The old man was King David, and he wanted to kill you because you destroyed his garden, his entire family. All of them, old and young, women and children, you have smitten and trampled to death. There remains but one small seedling, the unborn child of my daughter Yaleta, and when you tried to destroy even that, the owner of the garden intercepted you. That was when he was going to kill you."

"I believe you, Chafni! Your interpretation is as true as the dream you have helped me to recall. Tell your daughter that when she gives birth to her child, I will prize it as one of my own. I will keep the promise that I made in my dream. And now, Chafni, change your clothing and return home. I will restore to your daughter all Chanina's property, that she may raise her child in honorable surroundings. Let me know immediately the fate of the child; I feel that my life is linked with his."

After a welcome bath and change of clothing, Rabbi Chafni was given one of the royal carriages, and he drove to the town where his daughter had been hiding. When he entered the lowly hut where she had found refuge, he found her lying on a bed of palm-leaves, and beside her was a healthy, newborn baby. This was the only surviving prince of the House of David! Rabbi Chafni offered his grateful thanks to G-d. A son had been born to the House of David! The day would yet come when a Jewish king would rule over the land of his ancestors.

Rabbi Chafni rushed back to bring the joyous news to the king.

"Let him be called Bustenai," the king said, "because he sprang forth from the *busten* (Persian for 'garden') of my dream!"

Thus new hope filled the hearts of the children of Israel. An heir had been born to the House of David!

Chapter Five

ustenai was growing up to be a healthy and handsome child. He was Yaleta's only consolation for the loss of her brave and noble husband.

One day a visitor came to Princess Yaleta's palace. It was Benjamin; he had come to visit old Rabbi Chafni. When Yaleta saw him, she again expressed her deep gratitude to him for having saved her life, but Benjamin would not listen. He replied that he had only fulfilled his duty to his comrade, to the House of David, and to the Jewish people.

For several days Benjamin remained as a guest in the princess's palace. He made a very favorable impression on Rabbi Chafni, who discovered that not only did the vistor come from an honorable family, but that he was also a pious scholar of unusually noble character. When Rabbi Chafni learned that he had recently lost his wife, he approached Benjamin and said: "Benjamin, my days are growing short. Only one thing prevents me from facing death with complete peace of mind. When I am gone, my daughter and her child will be alone in the world. If she would have you for a husband, I could die in peace."

Benjamin had often had this same thought in his mind, but he had never dared to mention it to the princess.

"It would make me very happy," he said, "to have the honor of taking the princess's hand in marriage. I would always try to make her life happy and would be a true father to her child."

Rabbi Chafni now went to inform his daughter of this proposal. She was sitting in the garden watching her son at play. Yaleta protested that she could not even bear to think that her father would leave her. In any case she did not want another husband. She would always be true to Huna although he was dead. Her father insisted that Benjamin, the good man who had saved her life, would be a loyal protector to her and her child.

While they were talking, Bustenai came to them, holding in his hand something that he took to be a colorful plaything. When he was close enough for them to see what it was, they both gasped in horror! It was a small, poisonous snake! The child held the reptile by the neck, which made it unable to turn its head and bite him. Rabbi Chafni quickly grabbed the snake, holding it similarly, and battered it to death against the ground. The princess clutched her child to her bosom, showered him with kisses and shed tears of relief.

"Do you still think that I need a protector?" she cried out. "Only the hand of the Almighty could have led Bustenai to grasp the snake in a way that it could do him no harm. I do not want a husband; I shall devote my life to my son. He does not need a protector; in him lies the hope of our people and G-d is his protector."

That same day Benjamin returned to Tiberias in the Holy Land.

Chapter Six

ustenai was developing into a lively, quick-witted boy. He showed a remarkable ability to comprehend and assimilate all he was taught. Rabbi Chafni gave up his position as head of the Yeshiva in Sura so that he would be free to devote himself to the training of the child. He also selected an orphan of Bustenai's age who showed similar talents, and who could be a comrade to the child. Bustenai and Achai, the orphan, soon became good and firm friends, and an unbreakable bond tied them to one another. The king had not forgotten his pledge. Rabbi Chafni often had to report to him on the child's health; once Kuzroi himself came to Mechuza to inform himself of the child's progress and welfare.

Under the guidance of Rabbi Chafni, the two children were taught in a manner that far surpassed the usual method of instruction. When the children were old enough, Rabbi Chafni began teaching them Chumash. Each time he reviewed the Chumash with them, he would explain the meaning of each word in greater detail and in greater depth. When they were ten, he began to teach them the Talmud. They quickly memorized the Mishnah, and Rabbi Chafni discussed with them the Gemorro that referred to it. Thus, at the age of fifteen, the two boys had a clear concept of the different subjects contained in the Talmud. Besides the interpretations of the Talmud and other holy works, Rabbi Chafni showed them how every letter of the Torah might hold a key to the secrets of the universe.

One dreaded day the king sent a message commanding Bustenai to come to the royal palace to live. The boy could not refuse, and now came the painful parting from his grandfather and his dear mother.

Rabbi Chafni, who loved Bustenai like a son, spoke words of advice to him before he left. The boy promised him that, although he would be living in the king's palace, he would never forget what he had been taught. The Almighty Who had protected him even before he was born, would shield him from the temptations of the king's palace.

"Then G-d be with you," Rabbi Chafni said. "Neither I nor your mother can accompany you, but your friend Achai will remain with you."

With tears streaming from his eyes, Rabbi Chafni blessed the boy and bade him farewell. Though great was the grandfather's sorrow at parting from the boy, that of his mother was far greater. Since her husband's death, her son was her only consolation. For her son's sake she had accepted the lonely life of a widow. Now he was leaving her! When would she see him again? Only her faith in the Grace of G-d eased the pain that filled her heart.

"O Almighty G-d," she cried, "it is Your holy will. Let it be so."

Chapter Seven

hen the two boys entered Destagerd, the Persian capital, they were fascinated by the unbelievable splendor of the city. As they rode through the streets, magnificent palaces rose on both sides. But they were also reminded of certin dark deeds committed by the king during the construction of this miracle-city, tales that were always heard in whispers.

Achai had relatives in the city, and it was at their house that the two boys intended to stay, until their own quarters were ready. Abun, Achai's uncle, greeted them warmly, honored to have the prince as his guest. Rachel, his wife, was glad to see how well her sister's child had fared, and she embraced Achai tenderly. They entered the house, where a festive meal awaited them.

The king had made elaborate preparations for Bustenai's reception. He sat on this throne, constructed of gold and diamonds, and around him were the royal family and the highest nobles of the kingdom.

When Bustenai entered, he was blinded by the brilliance of the room, but he soon recovered and prostrated himself before the king.

"Arise," the king commanded. "By what name are you called?

"Bustenai, Your Majesty."

"Do you know who gave you that name?"

"Your Most Gracious Majesty."

"Do you know why that name was given to you?"

"Your servant knows."

"Have you also been told that your father had to be executed?"

Rabbi Chafni had told Bustenai the true story of his father's heroic death, but he had warned the boy neither to seek revenge or incure the king's displeasure.

"My grandfather told that to me."

"And what do you have to say to it?"

"It was the Almighty's will."

The king was pleased with Bustenai, both with his appearance and his unhesitating manner of answering questions. The entire room was silent for a few moments, as the king surveyed the young man standing before him. Suddenly the stillness was broken by the buzzing of a mosquito that circled about the king's head. An attendant brushed it away, and it flew towards the other nobles who also motioned with their hands to scare it away. Then it landed on Bustenai's forehead. Statue-like, he did not move a muscle. He stood there, while the insect dug into his skin until an inflamed swelling appeared on his forehead.

The young princess Dara gasped as she stared at Bustenai. The king, who had been watching Bustenai very closely, admired his endurance, and asked him why he had allowed himself to be stung.

"My grandfather taught me," replied Bustenai, "that in the presence of a ruler, one should stand at attention and raise neither hand nor foot, except by leave of the king."

"You have been very well brought up," the king said. "Your father would still be alive if he had conducted himself as well. Now I am going to keep the promise that I made in my dream. You shall live in my palace, and you shall be treated like one of my own children. Your food will be prepared by a Jewish cook, for I know that you may not eat with us. I shall do great things for you if you are loyal to me. You will inherit the honors of your grandfather Chanina, and you will be appointed the 'Resh Galuta,' the Jewish leader of the Diaspora. One thing more; your coat of arms will bear the image of a mosquito."

Chapter Eight

pon returning to Abun's house, Bustenai bade his kind, friendly hosts, farewell. Achai could no longer live with him, but Bustenai promised that he would come to see him as often as possible. Bustenai then took up his residence in the king's palace.

In the palace, the king presented him to the royal family. Bustenai was introduced to Queen Shehrin, to the princess Artsim-Dakt and the prince Shiruya, who were children from a different wife, and to the fourteen year-old princess Dara, the queen's daughter. The king and Bustenai discussed various matters; the older princess and the prince left, and later the king and queen also rose to go. Bustenai remained with the young princess Dara.

As soon as they were alone, the princess began asking Bustenai about his religion. At first he was reluctant to talk about it, but since she seemed eager to hear what he had to say on the subject, he told her about the one G-d in whom Jews believe: one G-d, Creator of the universe. He told her how the people, who had become wicked, forgot their Creator and worshipped many gods, and how Abraham had recognized the foolishness of idolatry and had spread the belief in the existence of one G-d wherever he went.

He went on to show her how humane the Jewish laws were, how just and equitable. He explained to her that the victories and conquests that had been gained by the heroes of Persia and other countries were really the work of G-d. The Jews had always realized this. They knew that everything happened because G-d willed it so.

Dara listened like one in a trance. Young though she was, she contrasted the Jewish religion with the hatred and lawlessness of her land. She marveled at the learning called the Torah, which had given this boy so much understanding. Lost in thought, she rose and walked about the garden, and Bustenai also absorbed in their talk, walked beside her.

Suddenly they were shaken out of their deep contemplation by the sound of the king's voice.

"I see, Dara, that you are making our guest feel at home here. That is good." Turning to Bustenai, the king said: "Tomorrow you will take part in the deer-hunt that I have arranged."

Although Bustenai's grandfather had taught him the use of the bow and arrow in case he should ever need it to serve the king, Bustenai tried to avoid participation in the killing of animals for no other reason than the sheer pleasure of the sport. However, when the king insisted, Bustenai realized that it was unwise to refuse and agreed to do the king's bidding.

The next day, amid the blasts of the trumpets and the barking of the hounds, the signal was given to begin the hunt. Soon afterwards, Bustenai spotted the giant deer, which had been held captive in the king's preserve and had now been freed for the purpose of the chase, running across his path. His first impulse was to kill the animal and show the king his skill in archery, but he quickly restrained himself. He had promised the king to join in the hunt, not to engage in the killing that was part of it. A few minutes later a blast of trumpets struck his ears; Muzdu, the highest noble in the land, had slain the deer.

The next moment the king appeared at the side of Prince Muzdu, shouting in a terrible fury:

"How dare you take the shot that belonged to me! You knave! How dare you take the king's first try!"

Muzdu made no attempt to disguise his anger as he replied:

"You brought us here to shoot, did you not?"

"Silence, slave!" the king roared. But Muzdu refused to be repressed.

"I am no slave; I am the highest prince in the land! Do you take me for the Jewish prince that you murdered!"

"Traitor!" screamed the king, beside himself with rage, and swiftly raised the bow that he held in his hand. He let fly an arrow that struck the prince in the throat. The onlookers gasped as the man fell dead at the king's feet.

"Burn his carcass," the king ordered, and he turned his horse about and rode towards Destagard.

Bustenai raised his eyes to heaven:

"Thank You, O Lord," he whispered, "for staying my hand from slaying the deer. I see now what would have happened to me had I dared shoot the deer!"

Chapter Nine

After the hunt, the royal family took a stroll in the royal garden. Princess Dara went in search of Bustenai, as she wanted to continue the interesting talk she had had with him on the previous day. She found him in a secluded nook, sitting under a cypress tree, looking very forlorn.

"Why do you look so sad, my friend?" Princess Dara said to him gently. Bustenai looked up, somewhat startled, awakening from his reverie.

"What is worrying you?" she continued. "Can you not hear the sweet strains of Barbud's singing? He is the greatest singer in Persia. Let his songs drive your melancholy away."

"Princess Dara," Bustenai began in earnest tones, "I had a terrible experience this morning. I witnessed a very shocking event indeed. Before my very eyes a person, one of the most prominent personages in the kingdom, was put to death mercilessly."

"But surely he had sinned against the king, and his death was therefore deserved," protested the princess.

"No, Dara, he certainly did not deserve to be put

to death. He was the victim of ruthless tyranny." Bustenai exclaimed with feeling.

"Hush, Bustenai! Do not say such things if you value your life! Someone might hear you!" Dara looked around fearfully, and continued in a low voice: "Why should you be so concerned about this fellow Muzdu? Did you know him at all?"

"No, I did not know him, but what has that to do with the matter? Yesterday, Muzdu was one of the most powerful and honored dignitaries in the land, a chosen friend in the king's exclusive circle; today he was shot down like a wild animal of the forest! His might, power, and honor, all gone in a flash. Muzdu also referred, a few seconds before his death, to my father who also was slain in cold blood. Naturally it has all affected me deeply."

"Do you hate me very much, Bustenai?" Dara asked.

"I, hate you?" exclaimed Bustenai. "How absurd! And why should I hate you, dear Princess?"

"My father was responsible for your father's death," replied Dara.

"And you believe I should therefore hate you? No, Princess, our Torah teaches us: 'Fathers should not die for the sins of their children, neither should the children die for the sins committed by their fathers. Each must be responsible for his own actions and misdeeds'."

"How beautiful are your laws!" exclaimed Dara.

"We Persians have laws very different from yours. In Persia it happens quite frequently that a whole tribe is wiped out because of the offense of one of its members."

While Dara and Bustenai were engaged in this serious talk, someone suddenly burst his way into the royal garden. The watchmen tried to stop him, but the intruder pushed them roughly aside. A wealthy Persian, he was not used to being dictated to by the ordinary rank and file. Having gained entrance into the garden, he looked around, and, seeing the king, he rushed up to him shouting hysterically:

"Help! O great king, help!" and he threw himself at the king's feet.

"Who allowed you to disturb the peace of my garden!" the king roared at him in anger.

"I forced my way in, O Your Majesty. I had to see you to seek your aid."

"Who are you?" the king asked gruffly.

"My name is Eryeh," the man replied, rising to his feet. "I belong to a distinguished and noble family that has dwelt in these parts for many years. On our estates which lie nearby, I have been living peacefully with my neighbors and very happily with my wife, Rudata, who has born me two beautiful sons. Each day, I humbly thanked the gods for having blessed me with fortune and a lovely family." As the king did not interrupt him, he continued:

"A few weeks ago, your son, Prince Shiruya, came

to us, tired and hungry from hunting. Naturally we received him as an honored guest. We gave him food and drink to refresh himself and made him as comfortable as we possibly could. We expected no thanks for what we did, but O, Your Majesty," his voice rose on a wailing cry, "today while I was away from home, Prince Shiruya forced his way into my house and kidnapped my beloved wife, the mother of our dear children."

"And for this, you have the effrontery to force your way into my garden and disturb my peace! What's all the fuss about! Take another wife!"

"Oh do not speak so, Your Majesty!" the man wailed. "My wife is dear and loyal to me, and our little ones are crying for her!"

"And because your brats are squawking, you dare to come and bother me, your king! Have I not done enough for my ungrateful subjects, by bringing you wealth and fame? Twenty battles have I waged for you, and brought you the fruits of victory, the riches won from all the vanquished nations!

"Prince Shiruya is my son, heir to the throne, and as such he has every right to your wives and daughters. There is a spirit of mutiny rising up among you which I shall not tolerate any longer! Muzdu has already felt the strength of my arm. I shall teach you all the same lesson!"

Turning to Tur, the Captain of the Guard, the king called out:

"Tur, come here!" The captain quickly ran forward and prostrated himself before the king.

"Replace the watchmen of the gate with others who are more reliable. And see that these untrustworthy ones who failed in their duty to guard the gates be put to death!"

Tur bowed low before the king, then hurried off to carry out his order. The king turned to Eryeh and said to him in a more conciliatory tone: "I shall be kind to you and not punish you for having forced your way into the royal garden. Go home and take another wife. As for your little ones, get them some toys to play with and they will forget their troubles. And as for my son, Prince Shiruya, leave him his plaything. Now go, and consider yourself lucky that I have dealt so leniently with you."

"I don't want your so-called kindness!" Eryeh shouted. "You, who practice injustice as your right! Kill me and be done with your kindness!"

The king turned white with anger, but called out to his attendants:

"Remove this man from my presence, but do not kill him!"

"I would rather die than live under such circumstances," groaned Eryeh, but the attendants dragged him away before he could say anything more.

Tur had just appeared to inform the king that his death-sentences on the luckless watchmen had been carried out, when a noise was heard coming from the distance. It grew ever louder, until it resolved itself into a heart-rendering wail, accompanied by the tumultuous rattling of many swords.

Seeing the king's inquiring look, the Captain of the Guard said:

"Your Gracious Majesty, these are all the members of the family of the traitor, Muzdu. All, that is, excepting his eldest son, Hermus, who managed to escape. But all the others are here, being led to their death."

A smile of satisfaction spread over the lips of the king. As the sound of the wailing receded, the delicate tones of the singer were heard in the garden. Oblivious to the terror and suffering of the innocent victims who had just come and gone, the king and his courtiers followed the sounds of the music with delight.

From the midst of the thick bush, which completely concealed him, Bustenai had seen all that had transpired. He threw himself upon the ground and burst into bitter weeping. "O Lord of the Universe," he prayed, "Deliver me from this horrible place! Must my eyes see and my ears hear things which I am powerless to alter? The king behaves like a wild animal, waiting to pounce upon any prey that comes within reach of his claws, so that he can tear him to pieces! I beseech thee O Lord, protect me from this demon's clutches! I turn to Thee, my sole Protector."

As Bustenai arose from his prayer, he looked out

and saw Princess Dara. He came out of his hiding-place and approached her.

"Where have you been, Bustenai? I have been looking for you everywhere! My father asked where you were. Come along! But wait! You have been crying! This is terrible. Nobody must see that you are unhappy about what has just happened! It could cost you your life! Wipe away your tears and come with me to the king."

Bustenai realized that the princess was right, and he thought to himself how lucky he was to have such a true friend in a place where he was ever in danger. He therefore tried to compose himself and appear tranquil as he accompanied Princess Dara to the king.

As they entered the king's chambers, the king was about to address Bustenai when Kuzroi was informed that a special messenger had just arrived from distant Arabia, bearing a letter for King Kuzroi.

The king ordered the messenger to be brought in immediately.

A man entered, in simple attire, a letter in his hand. He bowed low before King Kuzroi.

"Who are you, and who sent you?" the king asked.

"My name is Seid," the man replied. "From the far deserts of Arabia have I brought a message from Mohammed, the prophet of Allah, to the king of Persia."

The king waved, almost imperceptibly, and his

secretary took the message and read it. When he had finished reading, he translated it aloud. It began with the customary salutation and blessings, but the important part of the letter read as follows:

"Know ye that the writer of this letter is the chosen prophet of Allah, Mohammed ibn Abdallah, and that I have been appointed by Allah to overthrow the idols of the people. He bids me command you to repudiate your false gods. Hear these words with fear for Allah has called to you! Unless you hearken to his words, your throne shall be taken from you, and your entire family shall be annihilated! Thus speaks Mohammed, son of Abdallah, of the tribe of Kireish."

The king and his courtiers greeted these words with loud guffaws of jeering laughter. The king carefully folded the letter several times and tore it into little pieces. Then he scattered them through the air like confetti.

"Mad!" he shouted to the messenger. "Tell the madman who sent you here what I have done to his letter. Tell him that if he dares to place his foot here, I will treat him the same way!"

The king's interpreter translated the king's words for the messenger. The Arab bowed low before the king, and quietly withdrew from the palace.

Chapter Ten

everal weeks passed, and Bustenai gradually accustomed himself to the life at the court. Were it not for the assistance of the clever young Princess Dara, he could easily have fallen a victim to the plots that were devised against him out of fierce jealousy. Prince Shiruya was too occupied with his own escapades and too engrossed in satisfying his desires to be concerned with the boy, but Bustenai had no respite from the intrigues and treachery of Princess Artsim-Dakt.

Bustenai eagerly looked forward to those hours when he could leave the court and go to Abun's house. There he would spend many delightful hours studying with Achai. Achai's uncle and aunt were so pleased with their nephew, that they had betrothed their only daughter to the young scholar. Since Abun was wealthy, he insisted that Achai should not seek employment; instead he would remain in Abun's house and devote his time to study.

Bustenai shared his friend's happiness, and he wished that he himself were fortunate enough to devote all his days to learning.

One day, when Bustenai came to Abun's house,

he was overjoyed to find that Rabbi Chafni had come to visit him. They embraced each other tenderly, and Rabbi Chafni brought him loving greetings from his dear mother and grandmother.

Bustenai clung to his grandfather and implored him to take him back home with him, where he could once again spend his time in peaceful study. Bustenai recounted to his grandfather the cruelty and strife of the court and the constant plots against him. How weary he was of it all! But Rabbi Chafni was powerless to help him.

After a pause, in which Rabbi Chafni regarded his fine grandson with loving pride, he said to him sympathetically:

"So you don't feel good at the king's court, that is a pity."

"Oh, don't worry about me, grandfather, I'll be alright! Though I must say that were it not for the loyal friendship of the young Princess Dara, my life would have been in danger more than once."

"My dear Bustenai," exclaimed his grandfather, "take care that you do not step out of one danger into another! Watch that young and tender heart of yours! Do not aspire to winning a daughter of King Kuzroi. For, even were he to consent to such a union at some future date, remember that you are a Jew and dare not marry one who worships idols!"

"Have no fear on that score, dear grandfather, I

promise you I would rather die than thus transgress against G-d's commandment!"

Rabbi Chafni urged Bustenai to tell him more of his life at court. Bustenai described the strange Arab messenger sent by Mohammed ibn Abdallah who had come to King Kuzroi and the laughter and derision that had greeted the letter.

Rabbi Chafni listened to the story with a serious expression on his face.

"Yes, I, too, have heard of this Ishmaelite," he said, "this 'prophet' who preaches a new religion that is based on the belief in one G-d. Over five hundred years ago it had already been revealed to Rabbi Shimon ben Yochai that a new religion would arise to oppose the religion of the Romans.

"The conflict between these two religions would prevent the annihilation of the Jews that might have occurred had Rome been permitted to rule the world. Perhaps this Mohammed is fulfilling the prophecy that was given to Rabbi Shimon. Steadily the world is coming closer to accepting the teachings of our Torah. In destroying idol-worship, the Ishmaelites will become great; but Israel will still be persecuted. Many years must pass before the other nations recognize the full truth of the Torah. But we must remain firm. The day will yet come when the children of Jacob will be secure."

Rabbi Chafni continued to speak to Bustenai for

many hours, filling him with new hope and renewed faith.

The following morning, Rabbi Chafni bade Bustenai a reluctant farewell, returning to Mechuza, where Bustenai's mother waited impatiently for news of her beloved son.

Chapter Eleven

ing Kuzroi had meanwhile been informed by his spies of Bustenai's visit to the house of Abun, and of his meeting there with his grandfather. He did not approve of Bustenai's going there and suspected some disloyalty to himself.

The king, therefore, brought his suspicion's to the queen. Princess Dara was in her mother's boudoir as the king said to the queen: "You know my dear, all the Jews hate me. And I believe that I am especially hated by our young Bustenai. Yet how could I expect it to be otherwise? For have I not destroyed all his family? I would be relieved to be rid of him too. The only thing that holds me back is the solemn oath I took in my dream not to harm him. However, I am going to put the boy's loyalty to a test."

Dara listened to every word although she gave no sign of being interested.

"Bustenai seems a nice boy to me," the queen said, and Dara could have hugged her mother in gratitude.

"We shall soon find out whether he's nice or not," the king continued with an evil look on his face.

"Tonight, at the banquet-table, I shall offer the youngster a goblet of wine which he will not dare refuse. Once intoxicated, he will soon reveal all the hate that is in his heart. Then I shall have ample reason for ridding myself of him forever!"

Dara shuddered at her father's horrible threat to her dear friend, and she determined to seek out Bustenai as soon as possible to warn him of the new danger hanging over his unsuspecting head.

When the court went into the garden for its usual afternoon stroll and to listen to the singing of Bardud, Dara quickly drew Bustenai into a quiet corner and said to him in an urgent whisper: "Bustenai, listen very carefully and don't interrupt. Your life depends upon these words. I know you hate my father for what he has done to your father and to all your family. You also hate him for his cruelty and injustice. Now listen carefully, for I dare not raise my voice. Tomorrow there is to be a great banquet at which my father says he is going to get you drunk. Then he expects to find out how much you hate him! So you see Bustenai, you must be terribly careful what you say! I have warned you!

"But, dear Princess, if the king gets me drunk, how can I help what I say or do? I am a youth entirely unused to strong drink?

"I wish I knew how to advise you," replied Dara unhappily. "The king is going to offer you a huge goblet of wine which you will not dare refuse."

"But Dara, if the king offers me *his* wine, I dare not drink it. It is forbidden by Jewish Law, and I would rather die than do so!"

"Now I begin to see a way out!" exclaimed Dara with relief. "As my father allows you to have kosher food, he will not press you to drink forbidden wine, *as long as you drink some wine!* See? Here is where we can have a plan."

"This is what I shall do, my friend. I will order one of my most trustworthy servants to put colored water in your wineglass. You will pretend that your drink has intoxicated you and, in a drunken fashion, you will say flattering things to my father, the king."

"Another thing which I must tell you is, that in order to test you thoroughly, the king will afterwards give you a beaker of spirits which are known to clear one from intoxication. So, after you have drunk the contents of the second glass, you must quickly feign to have recovered and become sober again."

"O Dara, you have truly saved my life!" exclaimed Bustenai gratefully. "How can I ever repay you for all your kindness to me!"

"Please don't speak of repayment, Bustenai. You are dearer to me than father, mother, sister, and brother." Dara hurried away looking very moved.

Bustenai, left with his thoughts, felt somewhat troubled by the implication of Dara's words. There could be no close relationship between Dara, an idol-worshiper, and himself!

The next evening, as Dara had predicted, the king's chambers were brilliantly lit, the tables laid with gold and silver, and the king's court were all assembled to partake of the banquet that had been prepared.

In the midst of the feast the king called to Bustenai, for whom kosher food and drink had been specially provided: "Bustenai I have kept my word. You are living in my palace and are treated as one of the household. Now I am sure that you will be glad of the opportunity to drink a toast to the health of your benefactor."

"By your gracious leave, O king, I shall drink your health with the kosher wine which is in my goblet," said Bustenai.

"Of course, my boy, that is perfectly in order," the king replied.

Bustenai raised his goblet to his lips with a prayer in his heart that Dara had managed to carry out her plan. In the instant that he took the drink, he realized that Dara, his faithful friend, had been true to her word. It was indeed water that he was drinking. He drank the goblet dry and immediately began to pretend to be drunk. He grasped the edge of the table with his hands as if to steady himself, swaying backwards and forwards in so droll a manner, that the king could not refrain from laughing.

'Well, Bustenai, tell me, do you like it here in the palace?" the king asked him.

"Why shouldn't I like it here," Bustenai drawled thickly.

"And do you think I am a good king?" the king further asked.

"Very g-goo' king, very goo'," Bustenai said in an even thicker voice.

The king looked very pleased and handed him a second beaker. Bustenai grasped it clumsily, spilling a few drops as he gulped down the contents. He quickly shook himself, pushed a stray lock of hair out of his eyes and gazed at the king, first stupidly, then wide awake, and said:

"Please forgive me, O noble king. What have I been saying? I am not used to strong drink. So please disregard anything disrespectful that I may have said in my drunkenness."

"You are a good boy, Bustenai. You have nothing to fear from me. There is no evil in your heart, and you shall always be safe with me."

Bustenai looked as relieved as he truly felt, thanking G-d for his deliverance from mortal danger.

Chapter Twelve

 A few days later, as Bustenai was hurrying across the palace courtyard on his way to his friend Acahi, he was stopped by Prince Shiruya and a noisy company.

"Where are you off to in such a hurry?" the prince asked him.

"I am going to the royal stable master Abun," replied Bustenai.

"Splendid. I shall accompany you," said Shiruya. "My Arabian steed is sick, and my father has given me permission to choose another in its place. And what may *your* business be with Abun?"

"My friend Achai, with whom I was brought up, lives with Abun," said Bustenai.

"What is Achai doing at the house of Abun?" further asked Shiruya.

"He is betrothed to Sarah, Abun's only daughter."

Shiruya's face showed a new interest as he said, "Come, let us get along."

Bustenai's heart was filled with a vague misgiving. He regretted having told the prince where he was going. He well knew the reckless nature of the prince and of his daring, boisterous companions. But it was too late now; he had already told him.

Bustenai's heart sank as they all rode off together.

"There is Abun's house," said Bustenai to the prince as they came in sight of Abun's residence. The prince prodded his horse with his knees, the horse shot forward so that the prince was the first to reach the house.

Suddenly he stopped short, his eyes opening in wonder and admiration. The most beautiful girl he had ever seen was standing on the threshold! He gasped and remained rooted to the spot, thunderstruck.

The girl's cheeks crimsoned as she felt the prince's glance burning through her. She turned to go into the house, and the prince found his speech:

"Please do not go," he urged her gently and pleadingly. "Do tell me who you are!"

"I am Sarah, Abun's daughter," she replied hesitatingly.

"You beautiful Jewess," exclaimed the prince, "you are as lovely as Queen Esther, our ancestress. Nay, you are lovelier."

As Sarah tried to make her escape in her confusion, the prince waylaid her, saying: "Stay! I extend the golden scepter to you."

Sarah was saved further embarrassment by the appearance of Abun, her father, who, seeing the prince and his strange entourage, said to him deferentially: "To what do I owe the honor of a royal visit to my humble abode? And what, pray, can I do for you, Your Highness?"

Sarah gratefully took advantage of their conversation and disappeared into the house, and the prince did not dare stop her in her father's presence.

Prince Shiruya told Abun that he had come to choose a horse, and so they made their way to the stables.

Meanwhile Sarah, scared to death, quickly packed a few things and hurriedly left home, seeking refuge with relatives in a distant townlet.

Any other girl would have been only too happy to have attracted the prince. But not Sarah. She was a Jewish girl and would not give up her Judaism even for the crown of Persia. Besides, she loved Achai dearly.

On the following day, Prince Shiruya again turned up at Abun's house where he learned, to his chagrin, that Sarah had gone to visit relatives in Ktesipon. He lost no time in getting to that town, but despite a very thorough search, there was no sign of Sarah. He quickly realized that he had been deliberately misled, and that Sarah had not gone to Ktesipon. He understood the reason for this ruse was the fear that Sarah would fall into his hands. He decided that the best thing for the moment was to keep silent and hold his counsel.

The fact that Prince Shiruya seemed to have lost

interest in Sarah did not entirely reassure her family. To be on the safe side they delayed the marriage for three months while Sarah was kept in hiding.

But the prince had not forgotten the beautiful Jewish girl for one moment. In fact, the prince's spies kept close watch on Abun's house and reported to him when Sarah was to be brought home for her marriage to Achai.

Meanwhile, Abun's house became a hive of activity in preparation for the great event. All the important Jews of Destagard, Bustenai among them, were invited to the wedding of Abun's lovely, only daughter.

The great day at last arrived. The guests were assembled in the garden of Abun's house. Soft wedding music was heard as Sarah's parents led the radiant bride to the wedding canopy.

There was a moment of hushed stillness. Every one present felt the sacredness of the moment as the young couple were about to be joined by the bonds of marriage.

Suddenly a loud crash broke the stillness. Prince Shiruya appeared with an armed band of followers. He brandished an unsheathed sword in his right hand as he swooped upon the startled bride, caught her around the waist with his left arm and was about to dash off with her. As she struggled in his vicelike grip, her parents began to scream in terror, but Achai hurled himself at the prince in order to save his dear bride. The prince struck out furiously with his sword, and would almost certainly have killed Achai, but in that moment Bustenai jumped upon the prince, snatched the sword out of his hand and plunged it into the prince's right arm, rendering him helpless.

Achai went to Bustenai's aid, but Shiruya's followers were too many for them, and overpowered our two young heroes. Amid the helpless cries of the onlookers, Achai and Bustenai were chained and led away, together with the fainting prince.

When they all reached the palace, the king was horrified to see his fainting and bleeding son, and demanded to know what had transpired. He ordered his servants to put the prince to bed; Achai and Bustenai were thrown into one of the palace-vaults which served as a prison.

Chapter Thirteen

n the following day, the king assembled all the princes of Persia and Media, his courtiers and counsellors. He told them the story of the previous day's events and asked for their advice in the matter.

Their verdict was unanimous: the death penalty for both Achai and Bustenai.

"I am perfectly willing to see the death penalty carried out in the case of Achai," said the king, "but I must remind you of that dream I once had, wherein I promised always to protect Bustenai."

"But, your Majesty," protested one of the highest princes, "surely you realize that in the circumstances you are released from your oath! Do not forget that royal blood has been spilled, and is not the blood of the prince the same as if your own royal blood had been spilled? No one dare shed the blood of the holy Sassan* and escape with his life! Such a criminal must surely die!"

The king was silent for a while, then he said: "Very well, the death penalty is to be meted out to

---

*Sassan was the founder of the Persian dynasty which bore his name, and which reigned for over four centuries (3986-4401). Kusroi was his descendant.

both culprits. Prepare the scroll, and I shall place my royal seal upon it!"

In the meantime Abun had regained some self-command after this terrible shock and dispatched a swift messenger to Rabbi Chafni in Mechuza. Both Rabbi Chafni and his daughter Yaleta set out quickly for Destagerd. They immediately went to see the king.

"Your Majesty," said Rabbi Chafni earnestly, "remember your oath! If you dare lay a hand upon Bustenai, King David will avenge himself for the death of his grandson!"

"I am free of my oath," called out the king. "It is not I who am sending Bustenai to his death, but the law of the land!"

"But it is you, O king, who have the right over life and death. It is within your power to reprieve Bustenai if you will!" pleaded the old rabbi.

"Well I do not wish to do so," exclaimed the king. "I would only succeed in making an enemy out of my own son!"

Yaleta then threw herself at the king's feet, crying:

"My lord, you have already killed my dear husband, my father-in-law, and all the members of my family. I have only my son left, dearer to me than life itself, and now you wish to destroy him too! Please I beg of you, spare the life of my child! Do not break the heart of a poor mother whom you already turned into an unhappy widow!"

These words of entreaty, which could have melted the heart of a stone, left the king completely unmoved. He turned away and ordered his servants to remove the old man and his weeping daughter.

As they were being led away, Rabbi Chafni turned to shout at the king: "I warn you, Kuzroi, that you will not escape the consequences of your wicked deed. If you persist in carrying out the death penalty against Bustenai, King David will know how to protect his only remaining descendant and punish you!"

King Kuzroi burst into derisive laughter, but in his heart he was deeply afraid. He recalled his dream and the promise he had made to the old man. If there was anything that could make an impression upon this royal tyrant, it was fear for the safety of his own person. He would readily have pardoned Bustenai, but he feared the anger of his son Shiruya who would surely use this opportunity for revenge upon his father.

Shiruya was the son of a Persian noblewoman who, alone of all his wives, had presented him with a son. According to Perisan law, this should have entitled her to become the queen. Instead, Kuzroi drove her away and made another woman his queen. From sheer anguish and bitterness, Shiruya's mother became ill and died. But before her death she cursed the king and threatened that her son Shiruya would avenge her death.

In the history of Persia such cases were repeated over and over again. Had not Kuzroi himself been compelled to flee from his own father who had suspected that Kuzroi would raise his hand against him? Since the death of Shiruya's mother, Kuzroi had always been afraid of the prince and was always careful to give him no cause for seeking revenge.

Chapter Fourteen

n order to shake off despondency into which his fears had thrown him, the king made his way to the queen's boudoir. He found Queen Shehrin together with her daughter Dara who was in tears. As soon as Dara saw the king, she threw herself at his feet sobbing and begged him to spare the life of her dear friend Bustenai. She could not live were he to die.

"O my father," she cried, "just because Bustenai acted so loyally in defending his friend's bride, would you take his life? Shiruya's wound will quickly heal, but the wound in my heart will remain forever if dear Bustenai is put to death!"

The queen understood the true depths of Dara's grief. Realizing how inconsolable Dara would be were she to lose Bustenai, the queen herself was overcome with sorrow. "Please," she pleaded with Kuzroi as she wept copious tears, "pardon this young man for my daughter's sake! For my sake!"

The king had never before denied Queen Shehrin anything, for she was his favorite. Now, with a ghastly expression, he shook his head saying: "My dear queen, this is something I cannot do. The highest court in the land, the court of the seven princes, has decreed that Bustenai must die. You know, too, that were I to refuse to support the decree, it would be an excellent excuse for Shiruya to rise against me . . .

"And you, Dara, do you really love Bustenai so much?"

Dara swallowed her tears as she replied feelingly: "I love Bustenai more than the light of the sun; more than life itself!"

"But don't you know that you can never be his wife?" the king asked.

"I know that. But all I live for is to see him happy. He is so wonderful, so good, so wise." Grasping the king's hand, she again broke into tears of anguish.

The king was moved despite himself. "Yes, it is indeed true that Bustenai is a very fine young man. I am quite fond of him myself, especially when I think how much more loyal he is to me than my own son. I can seen now how much he means to you, Dara, and to you too, queen of my heart. Perhaps we shall yet find a way of saving our young friend."

Dara hurled herself at her father, laughing and crying at the same time. She was overcome with relief and joy at her father's words of hope, hope that her dear friend's life would be spared.

Chapter Fifteen

eanwhile, Bustenai and Achai languished in a dungeon deep in the bowels of the earth.

"Because of me, dear Bustenai," said Achai bitterly, "you, too, must lose your life. It will be my fault if the House of David will be wiped out forever. Woe is me, why must it be so!"

"Do not grieve so, Achai, You know full well that I would do the same thing again under similar circumstances. But do not despair for I still have hope that salvation will reach us somehow. G-d promised my ancestor King David that his house would never be destroyed, and I am the last surviving member of the House of David. Say, don't you hear footsteps approaching? See! The door is opening — The King!" They both fell to the ground before the king.

"Arise, Bustenai," called out the king. "I want to speak to you."

Bustenai arose and said to the king: "O king, I had to do what I did to save my friend's bride from a brutal assault."

"No matter," replied the king sternly. "You have shed the holy blood of Sassan, and for this you must die." Bustenai remained silent.

"My child," the king said more gently, "you have become dearer to me than my own son Shiruya. Why did you put me in this awkward position? I had no alternative but to sign your death-sentence!"

"Your Majesty, surely the king can find a way of granting pardon if he only wishes to do so," replied Bustenai.

"But this time it is impossible," protested the king. "If I were to pardon you now, Prince Shiruya would become my life-long enemy, and would indeed make an attempt on my life. Do you know who would grieve the most for your death?" the king asked.

"My dear mother, of course. Likewise my dear grandfather Rabbi Chafni, as well as many of my fellow Jews. They would all mourn my death," replied Bustenai.

"More than all these, Bustenai, would my little daughter Dara weep for you. You look surprised. It is true that the only daughter of my beloved queen Shehrin, loves you."

"And what may your purpose be, O king, in telling me this now? Is it to make death even more bitter than it is?"

"Aha! So you love her too?"

"How could I, your humble servant, aspire to the hand of the daughter of Your Majesty."

"What if Dara were a Jewess?" the king further asked.

"Then I would consider myself the luckiest of

mortals were I to win her. Even if she were but a poor maid, I would raise her to the highest pinnacles of nobility, so great is my love for her."

"My dearest child, let me embrace you," cried out the king. "I shall see to it that the physicians cause Shiruya to die of his wound. Then you shall, in truth, be my heir and shall reign after me. Come to my arms! Let me kiss you!"

But Bustenai did not stir. "My lord," he said, "you surely do not believe that all the nations under your rule will be ready to serve a king who refuses to worship their idols?"

"You foolish boy," laughed the king. "Naturally you will have to pretend publicly that you, too, serve the gods of the Persians. Secretly you can worship your own Jewish G-d faithfully!"

"I shall never for a single moment deny the existence and omnipotence of our one and only true G-d, the Creator of heaven and earth!"

"You really are speaking foolishly," protested the king. "When you become King of Persia, you will have the power to command all your subjects to serve your G-d. Until that time, naturally, you will have to bow down to our Persian idols."

"No indeed," cried out Bustenai vehemently. "That I will never do!"

"Then die, you silly child!" the king answered angrily.

"Very well, I shall die." said Bustenai.

The king went out, but returned a moment later, leading Dara by the hand. "My daughter," he said, "I have offered Bustenai a pardon, life instead of death, and you for a wife. Yet, he says, he will rather die."

"I choose death only because I refuse to deny my G-d, the G-d of my fathers!" cried Bustenai.

"Dear Bustenai," said Princess Dara tearfully, "my father told me that he will make you king after him. You will rule over all Persia with me as your wife. Think of the glorious future that lies ahead of us. Think of how we shall together be able to help all the nations who will be under us. With your great wisdom you would be able to make new and wiser laws for the country and people. Surely for such a future, it is worth making some sacrifice!"

"Dara, why must you join those who would torment me? You offer me life, a kingdom, nay, you offer me the world in offering me your dear self. But dearer to me than all else are my G-d's laws, and He commands me: "Choose death rather than the worship of idols! I am ready to die, Dara."

"Then die you shall, you foolish Jew," cried out King Kuzroi in a rage. "But I am free of the oath I gave in my dream, to protect you!" He led the tearful Dara out of the dungeon.

That very day, the king attached his royal seal to the death sentence of Bustenai.

Chapter Sixteen

When Dara returned to her mother's boudoir, she threw herself down in despair before her. "Mother dearest, all is lost," she said. 'My heart is broken, yet I cannot help admiring Bustenai's unfaltering faith in the face of all temptation. He refused even to appear to follow our religion. Nothing would he do against his G-d and religion. I must lose him," she ended hopelessly.

"He is much finer than I, Dara," replied the queen. "I was born to a faith that eschewed idol-worship, yet I gave it up to become a queen. I was born in Pelusium and was to have married a very fine man, but unfortunately he died. When Pelusium was captured, I was one of the captives carried off and brought here. Ferhad, a renowned architect was building this city at that time. He fell in love with me and was prepared to become a Christian and marry me. We were to have emigrated to Constantinople where we could have lived in the Christian faith of my parents. Ferhad was such a fine man, and I loved him too. He showed me all the plans he had drawn for the building of this city." The queen was glad to see that

Dara was making an attempt to listen with interest and trying to shake off her misery.

"Yes, my child, Ferhad was a clever man. He said to me: 'One never knows with a king. Today you can be his favorite and the next day you find you have displeased him and he throws you into prison!' Ferhad built a secret passage underground, leading out of the palace prison into the open beyond. He wanted to safeguard himself, but the poor man died anyway. But what am I saying, Dara? Did you hear? Listen, we can yet save our young friend! I know the secret of this underground passage that Ferhad built and told me about!"

Dara was quite awake now to the implication in her mother's words. Bustenai could be saved! There was no time to be lost!

"Thank G-d!" cried the queen, "I remembered in time! Ferhad told me exactly how to find the entrance into this secret chamber in case he should ever be imprisoned, and then we could escape together."

"And dearest mother, do you really know the secret? It seems almost too good to be true! Tell me quickly, what can we now do?"

"Listen carefully, my daughter. Take our old Arab servant, Suleika. She is my loyal friend and would never betray us. Let her take a lamp to light up the secret corridor leading into the open, and so Bustenai and his friend will be able to make their escape.

"Take this royal signet-ring with you in case of trouble. I believe the sentry at the prison entrance will allow you in, as he has already seen you taken there by the king. If he creates any difficulty, show him the royal ring, and he will allow you to pass without further question. When you enter the dungeon, you will see that the walls are built of huge square stones. Beginning from your left, count twenty stones and you will find that the twentieth stone can be moved with a little effort. One stone above this stone and two stones below, are also movable. When these stones have been removed, there is sufficient opening for a person to crawl through. The opening leads into a narrow corridor which grows ever wider until you reach a door which has a key in the lock. All you have to do is open this door, and you have gained your freedom."

Dara repeated the instructions until her mother was satisfied that she had it all clear. Dara kissed her mother and went off to prepare for the rescue.

Chapter Seventeen

As soon as the king and Dara had left the dungeon, Bustenai threw himself to the ground in a fit of weeping. Achai's heart was heavy, yet he tried to find the right words to cheer his dear friend.

"My dear Bustenai," he said to him. "Do not weep, for it is a great sacrifice you have made today. Had you lived a hundred years, you could not have shown more faith in G-d than you have now done. You have given up love, freedom, a kingdom, even life itself. Truly it is a privilege to die together with such a hero and Tzadik as you, my friend."

"But, Achai, don't you realize that with my passing, the last surviving member of the House of David will be gone!"

"The Almighty can save him whom He wishes, no matter what the circumstances," answered Achai earnestly.

No sooner had these words left his lips than a noise was heard behind the prison door. The door opened slowly and there on the threshhold stood the princess Dara with the Arab servant Suleika behind her.

Bustenai sprang to his feet. "Dara!" he cried.

"You have come to bid me a last farewell. Are you not angry with me?"

"And why should I be angry with you?" replied Dara gently. "You were very dear to me when I loved you for the boy you were. But having seen you make sacrifices that even few grown men would have the courage for, my love and respect for you are boundless; I salute you most humbly."

"Wonderful Dara! Why must I be called upon to die before I have even had a chance of repaying you for all your goodness!" exclaimed Bustenai.

"You are not going to die, Bustenai. I am here to save you and your friend." Incredulous and stunned, Bustenai and Achai gazed at Dara who began to count aloud the stones of the wall and as she reached twenty, she pushed that stone and it moved, revealing a hole. She removed the stone above it and also the two stones beneath, and the complete opening was there.

"This," said Dara, "is where you make your escape. Suleika will take this lamp and light the way for you through this pasage. When you get to the end of the corridor, you will reach a door which has a key in the lock on the inside. Unlock this door and step out into 'freedom.' Suleika will lock the door after you and return to me here. We will replace the stones in the wall, and no one will ever know how you made your getaway. Do not worry; Suleika is loyal to us and will not betray us."

"But, dear Dara, how did you manage this wonderful thing?" asked Bustenai in amazement and relief.

"There is no time to talk about it now, Bustenai. My mother had the secret from the architect of the palace — but never mind that now. Let us rejoice that you and your friend are safe. Do not go to Mechuza because they are sure to search for you there."

"Dara, how can I run away, leaving you to bear the blame for our escape?" protested Bustenai.

"My mother and I are the only people who know of this secret passage, and as I said, Suleika can be trusted to guard our secret. You have nothing to fear, but you must hurry, beloved. There is no time to be lost for your death sentence was to be carried out early tomorrow morning."

"Very well, dear princess. I cannot say 'thank you,' for mere words cannot express the goodness you have shown me. I pray to G-d that He will one day permit me to repay you in full measure for all you have done for me. Goodbye, dear Dara, I shall never forget you. G-d bless you always."

Suleika was already through the hole and in the corridor, with Achai behind her. Bustenai was about to follow, when Dara pushed a heavy bag of coins into his hand, saying: "Take this, Bustenai. You will surely have need of it."

"Thank you Dara again," called Bustenai as he went through the hole in the wall. "Thank you a thousand times! G-d bless you and keep you safe and well!"

"G-d bless you, too, my dearest friend. Goodbye, Bustenai, goodbye." Dara could barely keep the sobs out of her voice, but she just managed to control herself.

Suleika was at the door at the end of the corridor. She oiled the lock and the key then turned. Suleika, without a word, opened the door and stood aside as Bustenai and Achai slipped through it, leaving death behind and going out to freedom and life.

"Goodbye, Suleika. Thank you, too. Take good care of Princess Dara." The two young men silently departed into the night.

Bustenai and Achai travelled all that night until the break of dawn. At daybreak they hid in a village, and only when darkness fell, did they again resume their journey.

On the following morning, the guard entered the dungeon to lead the prisoners to their doom, but to their astonishment they found the prison cell empty!

When they reported the matter to the king, Kuzroi exclaimed:

"It surely was King David who rescued his grandson Bustenai and his friend! He must have taken them through the thick stone walls of the prison. There was no other way . . ."

When Rabbi Chafni and his daughter Yaleta heard of the escape, they, too, believed that King

David had saved Bustenai. They returned to Mechuza, thanking G-d for His boundless mercy, and awaited Bustenai's coming. But Bustenai did not come. Months later they received word by special messenger that Bustenai and Achai had the good fortune to cross the Persian border into safety.

Chapter Eighteen

ing Kuzroi's attention was diverted from Bustenai by events of high import occurring in the Eastern Roman Empire, Persia's long-standing rival for dominance of Asia Minor.

Heraclius, considered a weak and ineffectual ruler, now wore the imperial crown. The Byzantine Empire was beset with grave dangers. From the north, the Avars, a warlike, nomadic tribe, had already overrun the northern borders of the realm and were threatening to beseige Constantinople. Kuzroi seized this opportune moment to simultaneously launch a Persian attack from the east on the city of Constantinople.

Heraclius's position was desperate. The outlying districts surrounbing Constantinople were already devastated. From the eastern borders, the Perisan armies pressed forward. Determined to avoid armed confrontataion at all costs, Heraclius's strategy was to conciliate rather than fight his adversaries.

Heraclius's first move therefore was to establish relations with the Avars. To Heraclius's great relief, the Avarian king agreed to meet for discussion. Heraclius gathered all his princes together and ordered them to dress with all due pomp and cermony, as befitted the glorious tradition of ancient Rome. He, too, arrayed himself in all his glory, his jewelled crown upon his head, his robes of silk and satin studded with diamonds, gold and silver.

Heraclius thought that the Avars, awed by this glittering display, would beg for peace and retreat. But when the Avars beheld the splendor of Heraclius's retinue, a very different feeling was kindled within them. The silks, satins and jewels inflamed their hatred and jealousy, and they immediately fell upon Heraclius's princes, killing them right and left and robbing them of their costly raiment.

Heraclius would have shared the same fate, but thanks to his fleet-footed steed, he made off in great haste and succeeded in reaching safety.

Heraclius then attempted to make peace with the Persians. The Persian commander-in-chief, Zain, received the Roman emperor with great ceremony and deference. He promised he would personally escort Heraclius' delegation, which consisted of a bishop and two distinguished generals, to Destagerd, where they could present their requests to Kuzroi.

When the Persian monarch learned what Zain had promised, his anger knew no bounds. "I want no envoys,' Kuzroi railed, "You should have brought me the Roman Emperor himself, in chains!"

The commander-in-chief was sentenced to death, and the Roman envoys were informed that King

Kuzroi would make peace with their emperor if he would agree to pay an annual tribute of sixteen million talents in gold, one and a half million talents in silver, a thousand silk robes, a thousand good horses and a thousand of the fairest women in the realm.

The emperor was furious at this rejoinder to his peacemaking attempt. He saw that there was no alternative but to fight the Persians in defense of the honor and existence of his empire.

Following the ancient Roman rule of 'divide and conquer,' Heraclius decided to appease the Avars by purchasing their good-will with gold. He sent them two hundred thousand pieces of gold, each worth sixteen talents. Free of one enemy, Heraclius devoted his energies to defending his kingdom against the Persian menace. First, he gathered all the treasures of his churches to raise money to wage war. He then strengthened and rebuilt the fortifications of his capital city, Constantinople, against a possible attack by the Persians. Assembling his troops and officers, the Roman emperor set sail for Asia to meet the Persian armies.

Whilst Rome was engaged in this life and death struggle against the Persians, the Jews in both dominions were living in terror for their lives. The Jews, a minority everywhere, were always the first victims in time of war, for they suffered persecution at the hands of both victor and vanquished. The Jews in the Land of Israel in particular, were now filled with fear, for they had supported Persia in its previous attack against Rome.

In the city of Tiberias in Israel dwelt Benjamin, the former general of the army of Israel, who had fought side by side with Mar Huna, and who had saved Yaleta's life when Kuzroi had annihilated Mar Huna and his entire family. Benjamin's affairs had prospered greatly, and he had become one of the wealthiest men in Judea. In order to conciliate the Roman emperor, avert blodshed, and win the friendship of the Romans, Benjamin accumulated a vast store of provisions of food and apparel with the intention of presenting them to Heraclius and his armies.

When Heraclius entered Jerusalem, the most prominent citizens of the city went forth to greet the Emperor. Among them was Benjamin, who invited the Emperor to come to Tiberias and dwell there in his home.

Heraclius was overjoyed at the unexpected warmth and enthusiam of the Jews for the Roman cause. He was not too proud to show his gratitude, and accepted Benjamin's invitation with many thanks.

En route to Tiberias with Heraclius and his entourage were two Jewish youths who had hitherto managed to escape public notice. But upon their arrival in Tiberias one of the lads presented himself to Benjamin, offering him his hand and saying: "How fortunate indeed am I to greet the man to whom I owe my life!"

Benjamin looked at him uncomprehendingly, and asked: "Who are you?"

"I am Bustenai."

"Bustenai! Is it really you? I held you in my arms when you were but a babe. Your father was my beloved comrade-in-arms, your grandfather is and shall always be a venerated friend! What are you doing here?"

Bustenai then related the whole incredible story of his adventures to Benjamin, who listened with rapt attention. As soon as Bustenai had concluded his story, Benjamin at once brought him before the Roman Emperor. Once again Bustenai repeated the tale. "My lord and Emperor," he said in conclusion, "my people have long suffered abuse and cruelty at the hands of the Persians. We impatiently await the moment when we can free ourselves of the oppressive Persian yoke. Deal with us justly, and we will repay you with loyalty and devotion!"

"What are your demands?" the Emperor asked.

"We ask nothing of you, O Emperor, only your protection, so that we may dwell in peace and security on our beloved soil. We will gladly sustain your armies, provide for all their needs, and assist you in every way we can."

"And I will rally the many Jews who live on the borders of the Persian territories," declared Bustenai.

"They will flock to the call of the royal house of my ancestor. Under the shield of David, we will combat the Persians with all the strength and courage we possess."

The Emperor commanded his scribes to draw up the pact suggested by Bustenai, and then inscribed it with the Imperial Seal. While the Emperor implanted a kiss upon a golden cross, and swore by it that he would never violate the pact, Benjamin and Bustenai kissed a Sefer Torah and pledged their fidelity to the Emperor.

As these negotiations were taking place, the Persians had organized a huge army to fight the Romans. When Heraclius led his troops into battle, he shrewdly manoeuvered the Persian forces into a position where the latter were forced to fight facing the sun. With the passing hours of day, the sun grew more and more brilliant, until the Persian troops, blinded by the radiance, were thrown into chaos. The disorder that reigned in the Persian ranks proved a boon to the Romans, who scored a brilliant victory on the battlefield. Thus, the same Heraclius who had been regarded as a coward, emerged that day as a great hero.

The Emperor returned to the Land of Israel in triumph, grateful to all the Jews for their invaluable aid, and, above all, to Benjamin of Tiberias.

The Persian armies fled in disorder from Jerusalem. The gates of the holy city were eagerly thrown open to the Roman Emperor, who was now regarded by the Jews and Christians as their benefactor.

The patriarch of the Catholic church, Modestus, and his priests went forth to meet the Emperor, and together they all entered the church. The Emperor, on entering, prostrated himself to the ground, kissing it with devotion.

Yes, the Emperor regarded himself as pious, but he chose to make his own laws where his pleasures were concerned . . .

Chapter Nineteen

On the summit of Mount Zion there was, at that time, a fortress. It was here that the catholic patriarch had arranged a feast, celebrating the Roman victory over the Persians. At the Emperor's request, Bustenai and his friend Achai, as well as Benjamin of Tiberias were also invited.

"You must have suffered terribly during the sixteen years you were under the heathen Persians," the Emperor said to the patriarch Modestus during the feast.

"Yes, indeed, Your Majesty, words cannot describe the pain and suffering we experienced during this terrible time. But now we thank G-d that a true son of the catholic church sits upon the throne in triumph over the heathens. May you succeed in rooting out all the enemies of the church forever," replied Modestus piously.

"I must now return to my capital, Constantinople, where the Persians will be preparing to attack. Before I leave, is there anything I can do for you Modestus?" asked the Emperor.

"Yes, Your Majesty. There is something I would ask of you, not for myself, but for the good of our church. My request, O Emperor, is that you destroy the enemies of your faith, and they are right in your midst!"

"And who are these enemies you speak of, Modestus?" asked the Emperor.

"They are the Jews! These same Jews who now claim to be your friends are the same who helped Kuzroi capture the holy city. They killed more Christians than did the Persians. Ninety thousand Christians then fell at their hands. They destroyed all your churches and defiled the holy images. They abused our monks and nuns. Ths victory of the Persians would not have been possible without the aid of the Jews. It is now in your power to avenge these crimes, nay 'tis your duty," ended the patriarch, his voice shrill with hate.

"Do you hear, Benjamin?" called out the Emperor. "Is it true what Modestus has just said about you?"

"O mighty Emperor," replied Benjamin, "it is true that we joined the Persian ranks, for we mistakenly believed that there lay our hope of salvation. Since Rome accepted Christianity, our history is one long record of persecution. We were continually tortured and oppressed because of our faith. We were misled into believing that the Persians who are pagans, would have no religious grievance against us, and would allow us to live and worship as we chose. But not for one moment did we take part in the brutal massacre that the Persians indulged in. While they were engaged in ravaging, killing, and plundering, we Jews gathered at the Western Wall to pray to G-d to end the bloody conflict."

"You lie, Jew!" cut in the patriarch angrily. "Your people slaughtered Christians like so many cattle."

"Did you see this with your own eyes?" Benjamin asked quietly.

"No, but I was fully informed of your misdeeds," replied the patriarch heatedly.

"And I tell you these people who told you this lied," coolly replied Benjamin.

"O, Emperor," thundered the patriarch beside himself with fury, "the impudence of these Jews is unbearable! This man dares to call the holy monks from whose lips I heard these tales, liars! Such insolence should not be allowed to go unpunished!"

"I am sure, my lord and Emperor, that you will not violate your pact with us," said Bustenai. "We have complete faith in your word."

"Your Majesty," quickly exclaimed the patriarch, "you are not bound by your word to these Jews. When you made your oath you were not aware of their treachery to the church. Now that you know of their wicked deeds, it would be a crime to allow them to go unpunished."

"But I swore on the holy cross," protested Heraclius feebly.

"I will absolve you of your oath," declared the patriarch. "I will take upon myself the burden of your sin and, through prayer and fasting, I will obtain forgiveness for the violation of your oath."

"How can you, who call yourself a 'servant of G-d' advise the Emperor to break his oath!" exclaimed Bustenai to the patriarch, "Do you think you can bribe the Almighty with prayer and fasting? He sees the deeds of men and judges them accordingly. You are no priest; you are but a foul murderer who, out of greed for our riches, would condemn a whole nation of innocent people to death."

"Cease your quarreling," interrupted Heraclius, "I have sworn and I shall not break my oath."

The patriarch, however, had no intention of yielding so lightly. On the following morning he called on the Emperor, accompanied by an impressive delegation of bishops, and addressed himself thus:

"Your Majesty, I hope you have reconsidered our talk of yesterday. Please reflect, Your Highness, that should the Persians return, the Jews will surely desert you again. We cannot allow them another opportunity to pillage our churches and to rob our holy treasures once again! By virtue of the authority vested in me, I have the power and do indeed absolve you of your oath."

Whilst the Emperor was wavering in uneasy indecision, the bishop of Gallilee addressed Heraclius with this plea: "Allow me to prove to you, O Emperor, that the presence of the Jewish nation constitutes a threat to your empire and your church. In the monastery of Mount Sinai dwelt a monk who became enamored of a Jewish maiden. He became an apostate and adopted the Jewish faith so that he might marry the girl. Now he calls himself 'Abraham' and preaches to the people. He professes to have visions of Abraham, Moses, Ezra and Hillel. He has many followers who are convinced of the truth of his word. If you protect the Jews as you have promised, they will estrange the people from you and from your church. Your victories have no meaning if you support the very people who reject your faith. You must punish the Jews so that they, and the rest of the world, may know that the Roman church stands supreme."

At a prearranged signal, the bishops brought in an old recluse. The man was wearing a tattered robe, his feet were bare, and he was sightless. Looking upon this poor, bearded, bedraggled old man, Heraclius was visibly touched. The blind man, a victim of Mohammedan persecution, repeatedly called out pitifully: "Beware of the circumcised!" He was referring to the Mohammedans who had robbed him of his eyesight. Heraclius, who knew nothing of the man's history, construed "the circumcised" to mean the Jews. So, when the delegation again appealed to him, the Emperor granted their request and immediately gave the order for an attack on the Jews.

Once again the unfortunate Jews were at the

mercy of a vicious enemy bent on destruction, plunder, and murder. In the ancient Jewish cities of Jerusalem, Hebron, and Tiberias, Jewish blood reddened the fields. Some Jews succeeded in escaping to the hills, while others fled to Egypt. The Holy Land had become an arena where wild beasts had been let loose upon the helpless Jews. Benjamin, Achai, and Bustenai fled to Alexandria in Egypt, where Benjamin settled with his family, though little was now left of his huge fortune.

Bustenai recalled all his grandfather, Rabbi Chafni, had taught him about the important role that Mohammedanism was destined to play in world affairs. He decided the moment was ripe to meet its leader, who professed to be a prophet and teacher of a new faith. Together with Achai, Bustenai left Alexandria and crossed the Suez land-pass that led into Arabia.

Chapter Twenty

Kuzroi passed many long, sleepless nights after Bustenai's escape. The mysterious disappearance of Bustenai convinced the king that Bustenai's ancestor, King David, had come to save the surviving member of the House of David. Kuzroi was equally convinced that King David would take revenge on him for his treachery towards Bustenai.

Kuzroi was constantly haunted by Rabbi Chafni's words: "G-d will avenge the House of David, and then you will have to answer with your life!" An ugly melancholy descended upon Kuzroi which nothing could shake off. He allowed no one near him except the queen. As his melancholy grew, so grew his cruelty and his tyranny. He suspected everyone of conspiracy against his person; his officers trembled before him. Kuzroi's deluded imagination knew no bounds, and even his most trusted servants and courtiers were now supsected by him.

The spectre of death haunted the king day and night. While Heraclius rode at the head of his troops and led them into battle, Kuzroi did not even dare to appear on the battlefield lest an enemy arrow pierce his armor. With Kuzroi in such a mood, the morale of his army lagged; on the other hand, the courage of the Roman troops, inspired by an emperor who shared with them the common dangers and discomforts of war, mounted ever higher.

The second year of the war found Heraclius in combat with a huge army which was besieging Constantinople. This time thousands of savage Avars, Russians and Bulgars joined the gigantic campaign against the Romans. When the Romans saw that the suburbs of the city were already destroyed, and that the city itself was in grave danger, the patriarch of Constantinople went to ransom the city from the enemy.

The Avars disrobed the priest of his costly and magnificent garments and sent him back into the city. Heraclius, aware of the desperate position of Constantinople, sent troop reinforcements to strengthen the defense of the city. The disheartened people of Constantinople took courage once again and fought the besiegers with renewed vigor. With every weapon at their disposal, with crude iron rods and stones, they forced the enemy back from the gates of the city. When the Avar fleet sank in the Black Sea, the Avars deserted the battle and left the Perisans to fight on alone.

Heraclius hit upon a plan that ultimately was to result in Kuzroi's downfall. A Roman spy was planted at Kuzroi's palace for the purpose of arousing Kuzroi's suspicions against his brave and devoted commander-in-chief Zabar. The susceptible Kuzroi was an easy prey to Heraclius's plot. In a short while Kuzroi dispatched an order to Kadrigan, second in command, ordering Kadrigan to behead Zabar immediately. Zabar, however, intercepted this order and embarked on one of his own schemes. He appended the names of many commanding officers to the dispatch; he then called a council of war before which he read aloud the order sent by Kuzroi.

Kadrigan was overcome with indignation at the ingratitude and perversity of Kuzroi, who could repay service with such treatment! The Persian officers were all equally outraged and unanimously agreed that Kuzroi was no longer fit to wear the Persian crown. They decided to negotiate for peace with Constantinople. The Persian siege was lifted; the army returned to Persia.

The Persians suffered still another humiliating defeat at the hands of Heraclius and his armies. An allied force of Roman and Turkish troops overwhelmed the Persians at the battle of Lake Hidekel. After this Persian fiasco, the victorious Roman armies marched through Persian territory unimpeded by any opposition.

For many days, Destagerd, the magnificent city Kuzroi had constructed with the abundant spoils of many wars, was the scene of Roman plunder and slaughter. This great city, the seat of the fairest and most precious of oriental treasures, was no more. In its stead lay ruins.

Heraclius continued his march until he was stopped by the flooding of the Arcah River. The Emperor was now compelled to withdraw to the city of Taurus to await the cessation of the rainy season.

Meanwhile Kuzroi, who had fled with his family to Ktesipon, grew more dejected and distrustful with each passing day. His officers were more afraid of him than of the fiercest enemy. Unable to endure Kuzroi's senseless intimidation any longer, twenty-two of the highest officers of the army approached Prince Shiruya with an offer of allegiance if he would seize the throne from the king.

"Your father rules the kingdom more harshly than any foreign tyrant," they said to Shiruya. "We therefore wish to overthrow him and have you crowned king in his stead." Shiruya had long waited for this precious moment. Complying with the wishes of the officers, Shiruya donned the purple robes of royalty, and appeared before the people as their king. The Persians were weary of Kuzroi and were glad to welcome any change. Shiruya initiated his reign with a flurry of bountiful deeds, promising the soldiers an increase in pay, and freeing all political prisoners. Then he concluded a peace-treaty with the enemy.

Great was the joy and relief of the Persians at the change. Their enthusiasm in acclaiming the new king was almost hysterical. The success of the coup d'etat was insured by the officers of the army who imprisoned Kuzroi in a dark dungeon.

Kuzroi now had more time than he wanted to be alone with his thoughts. Memories of his past glory came to plague him, and he became aware of a new torment. With the realization that he himself had been the cause of his downfall, his conscience awoke and brought him gnawing regrets of the outrages he had committed. He thought of the hundreds of innocent people who had perished by his sword. The ghosts of all these people whom he had once tortured, imprisoned, or killed in fits of wild anger — all now flocked about him and jeered at him until he thought he would go mad!

After the first flush of joy subsided, the population of Ktesipon remembered their old king. They were filled with pity and sympathy for the sorry plight in which he now found himself. As soon as Shiruya sensed the change of heart in his people, he decided it was time to have his father "removed." Summoning Hermus before him, Shiruya cunningly goaded him to commit regicide. Had not Kuzroi killed Hermus's noble father Muzdu in a wild fit of anger, without justification? Here was Hermus's chance to seek revenge. As a further inducement, if any were needed, Shiruya offered him the Queen Shehrin for a wife. Hermus jumped at this proposition and eagerly accepted this bloody mission.

With an unsheathed sword in his hand, Hermus

descended into the dark dungeon where Kuzroi was held prisoner. Upon hearing Hermus's footstep, Kuzroi looked up, startled. "Do you know me, Kuzroi?" asked Hermus.

"Are you David, come to avenge the crimes against your descendants?"

"No, I am not David, but nevertheless I seek revenge," said Hermus.

"Who are you then?" called out Kuzroi in fear.

"I am Hermus, the son of Muzdu, whom you so cruelly murdered! I have come to avenge my father's untimely death."

Kuzroi fell grovelling at the feet of Hermus, crying incoherently for mercy. Recovering some presence of mind Kuzroi demanded of Hermus: "Are you not afraid to shed the royal blood of the holy Sassan?"

Hermus did not deign to reply but swooped upon Kuzroi, and with one swift stroke of his sword, felled the king's head.

Thus died Kuzroi, the once mighty monarch of Persia.

Chapter Twenty-One

riumphantly, Hermus returned to report his success to Shiruya. He would have liked to have shown him his sword, still crimson with the blood of Kuzroi, but the Persian law forbade him to appear armed in the king's presence.

"May all your enemies perish as did that bloodthirsty tyrant," Hermus said to Shiruya, who received the news with inward relief.

"I thank you, Hermus, for all you have done. From this day on, you shall be reckoned the first noble in the entire realm, just as your father was. His title, position, and great fortune will be restored to you. Tell me, Hermus, how did you carry out my mission?"

Hermus waxed quite eloquent in his endeavor to paint the scene as vividly as possible for Shiruya. When he related how he informed Kuzroi that he had come to avenge the death of his father, a diabolical grin appeared on the face of Shiruya as he said: "Do you realize, Hermus, that I find myself in exactly the same position as you did?"

"W-What do you mean?" stammered Hermus, suddenly scared.

"You are my father's murderer, are you not?" answered Shiruya. "And as you yourself have remarked, 'it is incumbent upon a son to avenge his father's death.'" As he spoke, the prince thrust a keen-edged knife into Hermus' heart before the latter realized Shiruya's intention. Hermus fell bleeding to the ground.

"A thousand curses upon you," groaned Hermus with his dying breath. A spurt of blood gushed from his mouth, and that was the end.

After Hermus's corpse was removed from his chamber, Shiruya summoned Shehrin to appear before him. The queen appeared looking very pale, but her eyes were red with obvious weeping.

"Do not weep, lovely Shehrin," he greeted her. "You shall be queen once again, queen of my heart and queen of my realm. Kuzroi no longer lives, but now you shall become my queen."

"You have killed him, you unnatural son!" cried out Shehrin contemptuously.

"You misjudge me, my queen," replied Shiruya soothingly. "It was not I who killed Kuzroi, but Hermus, who forced his way into the dungeon to avenge his father's death."

"But it was at your command," said Shehrin in anger.

"Surely it could not have been at my bidding, for look, there lies the knife with which I punished Hermus for his wicked deed. But let us turn from such gloomy discussion. Listen, Shehrin, there is a request I would make of you."

The queen was silent a moment, then she said slowly: "What do you want?"

"Please marry me. I want you to become my wife."

"Shiruya! How can you wed your father's widow!"

"Our laws permit it."

"Never!" cried Shehrin. "I was not raised in your idolatrous ways, and I will never submit to such an outrage!"

"You defy me bravely, Shehrin, but I warn you that there are ways and means of compelling you to obey my wishes."

"You may kill me, Shiruya, as you have killed so many others. I prefer death to a life of such depravity."

"No, Shehrin, I will not harm you. You need not expect death, but it is your daughter Dara who will die if you refuse to become my wife."

"Would you murder your own sister?"

"Would you be a party to the murder of your own daughter?"

Sobs shook Shehrin, who could no longer control herself.

"Very well, Shiruya," she finally said, "for my darling Dara's sake only, I agree to become your wife. But first of all you must swear to me by all that is dear and holy to you that you will guard Dara's life as if it were your own!"

"Gladly, dear Shehrin," replied Shiruya, and he knelt before the chief Persian deity, pronouncing the most solmen and weighty oath he knew, and promising he would protect Dara from harm as long as he lived.

He had scarely concluded when Shehrin grasped the knife that lay on the ground, and plunged it into her bosom.

Shiruya stood there, petrified.

"I am dying, Shiruya," gasped the queen. "Remember your oath . . ."

Shiruya threw himself over the body of the dying queen and cried in despair: "Why did you do this terrible thing, dearest Shehrin! I would have treasured your every wish, had you lived. I promise you, I shall keep the promise I have just made to you." Shiruya lay there motionless, yet more moved than he had ever been before.

Chapter Twenty-Two

ot much time was allowed Shiruya for personal grief. His great empire was on the verge of collapse or disintegration, if steps were not taken immediately to preserve it. The first thing Shiruya did was to negotiate a peace treaty with the Romans. He sent his emissaries to Taurus, where the Emperor had established his headquarters. Heraclius was delighted. He regarded this truce as most opportune, for the Avars and Bulgars were besieging Constantinople, and his presence was urgently needed there.

After Shiruya had rid the land of the Roman menace, he embarked upon a vigorous campaign to ease conditions in his kingdom and to establish the rule of law and order. For eight months Shiruya's rule was so exemplary that the people hoped that he would turn out a better king than they had anticipated. But Shiruya was not equal to their hopes. His weak character got the better of him, and he returned to his life of self-indulgence.

As we have already seen, Shiruya had a great weakness for women, and now, in his privileged position he felt he was free to do as he liked. Following the example of his ancestor, King Ahasuerus, Shiruya ordered all the pretty young women and girls in the kingdom to be brought to him. This decree so enraged the princes and nobles of Persia that they banded together and plotted to depose their shameful king. In a surprise attack upon Shiruya, the nobles killed him, putting his sister, the princess Artsim-Dakt, upon the throne in his stead.

This change of rulers boded no good for Princess Dara. She had lost her father and darling mother. Shiruya, who had vowed to protect her was also dead. Worst of all, the throne was now in the hands of her sister, Artsim-Dakt, who had always hated her.

Artsim-Dakt was an ambitious ruler. It plagued her to reflect that the Romans now ruled over many of the provinces which had belonged to Persia in her father's time. The longer she thought about it, the more determined she became to get these provinces back under Persian sovereignty.

To this end she entered into a pact with the Khan of the Tartars, a barbaric tribe, to join forces against the Roman Empire. The Khan agreed to help fight the Romans and, as a pledge of good faith, demanded that Princess Dara be given to him in marriage. Artsim-Dakt gave her consent to his request.

The queen summoned Dara and declared that, for the sake of Persia's future, she, Dara, must become the wife of the Kahn of the Tartars.

"Oh no!" cried out Dara in horror. "You surely do

not mean to place me at the mercy of such barbarians!"

"Where the welfare of our beloved country is concerned, I would hesitate at nothing. We must protect ourselves against the Romans, and this we can only do with the help of the Tartars. Since the Khan makes his help conditional upon your marrying him, you have no alternative but to marry him."

"But you are my sister! Have you no pity in your heart for me? You know what savages these Tartars are! Please, please do not ask this of me!" cried Dara.

"Selfish girl!" retorted Artsim-Dakt with scorn. "You ought to be proud to sacrifice yourself for the welfare of your country. But that requires a nobility of character which you, apparently, do not possess."

"This is not true!" protested Princess Dara. "Gladly would I die for my country. But you want me to submit to a life of torment which is infinitely worse than death! You ask the impossible!"

"I suppose you would have preferred to marry the Jewish boy who used to dwell at the palace. Now you are my subject and must obey my commands."

Dara threw herself at her sister's feet and implored her mercy: "I do not speak to you as my queen, but as my sister. When have I ever done anything to hurt or wrong you in any way! I am the only relative you have left in the world. You and I are the sole survivors of the House of Sassan. Treat me as your sister, not your subject, and preserve me from falling into the hands of the Khan of the Tartars. I could not stand it! I would rather die!"

Despite herself, Artsim-Dakt was moved by her sister's despair. "Very well," she said. "I shall inform the Khan that you refuse to marry him. But in order to appease his wrath, we will pretend that I am trying to force you to wed him. We will conceal you in a remote fortress. The Khan will be told that we have imprisoned you and that he will have to be patient until I can force you to change your mind."

Dara shed tears of gratitude and relief. "Oh dear sister," she exclaimed. "I would rather spend the rest of my days in the dismal solitude of a fortress than with that hateful, savage Tartar!"

Chapter Twenty-Three

uring the time that the Persian empire was at its lowest ebb, the Germanic peoples on the continent were growing in size and influence. A wave of anti-semitism swept their great empire as these barbarians sought to prove their loyalty to the Roman church by persecuting and oppressing the unfortunate Jews.

In the East, too, as a result of the destruction of both the first and second Temples by the Babylonians and Romans, many Jews had migrated to Arabia. When Persia, under whose benevolent rule Jews had dwelt in honor and liberty for more than one thousand years, became yet another oppressor, increasing numbers of Persian Jews turned to Arabia as a haven of safety and freedom.

The Jews who lived in Arabia felt a great affinity between themselves and the Arabs. They were both descended from Shem, and their languages were very similar. Relations between the two nations had always been of the friendliest kind. But a new turn of events changed all this.

In the tribe of Koreish, a young man called Mohammed worked and lived. Mohammed, the son of Abdallah, was an ignorant, illiterate Arab. Mingling freely with the Jews who dwelt in his village, Mohammed became acquainted with Jewish customs, religion, and history. What impressed him above all else in the Jewish law, was the oneness or unity of G-d Mohammad, who had known only the hundreds of deities that cluttered the Arab temples, undertook the founding and preaching of a new faith, whose god, Allah, was one and whose prophet was none other than himself. At first Mohammed was persecuted for his teachings, and he made little progress. His proselytes were mostly drawn from the lower classes. But as time passed, the people began to regard Mohammed as a true prophet, and he came to be recognized as the leader of the Arab people. The multitudes flocked to his banner, and he soon assembled vast armies of faithful followers.

Mohammed was very resentful of the fact that his religion was based, to a great extent, upon the Jewish religion. In order to obliterate every memory of what he owed to Jews and of all that he had taken from their laws and traditions, he began a systematic campaign of terror against the Jews — a bloodthirsty program. He gave the Jews the choice of two alternatives: they could either adopt his new faith and live unmolested and secure in Arab territory, or be driven out of Arabia, naked and penniless, relinquishing all their possessions in the hands of the Arabs. There was no guarantee, either, that they would not be slain in cold blood.

One peaceful Jewish community in the valley of Vadil-Kara had remained undisturbed by Arab violence. But one day the dreaded messengers of the Arab ruler presented themselves in the village. The peace-loving inhabitants gathered in council upon a hill, in order to decide what answer they should give the messenger, who said to them:

"Think carefully before you give your answer, Jews. Reflect upon the fate that awaits you if you dare to defy Mohammed. You know what has happened to your brethren. Our powerful Allah has crushed all who have opposed him, and he will not spare you either."

A murmur arose among the circle of Jews as the messenger finished speaking. In the general confusion, no one noticed two young men who lingered on the fringe of the crowd.

"My friends," called out Barak, the leader of the Jews in the valley, "let us depart and leave our worldly goods in the hands of the Arabs, so that we may continue to worship G-d and obey our Torah."

"But where can we go?" demanded Telek, another elder of the Jewish town. "Rome persecutes us, Persia oppresses us, and Arabia exiles us. We have no place to go, and no one to whom we can turn. Now that even the royal House of David has been destroyed, what hope is there left for us? Let us accept Mohammed's faith and at least live in peace!"

A dead silence fell upon the unhappy Jews at these terrible words. They could not bring themselves to accept Telek's proposal, yet they were powerless to refute his arguments.

"How do you know that Bustenai was killed?" inquired Barak.

"I have a very close friend who lived at the palace, at the time Bustenai was sentenced to death because he had wounded the prince in defense of a Jewish girl."

One of the two young men, who had taken no part in the discussion up to now, suddenly sprang forward. It was Bustenai himself.

"Permit me, a stranger among you, to inquire if your friend actually saw Bustenai put to death?"

"No," replied Telek, "my friend left the palace on the very day that the death sentence was issued."

"My brethren," cried out Bustenai in a mighty voice, "that death sentence was never executed! The Almighty rescued the last member of the House of David from under the gallows! He stands before you now! I am Bustenai!"

"Praised be the Lord!" cried the Jews ecstatically. "The Almighty has not forsaken us! Long live the House of David!" Bustenai was acclaimed on all sides.

Telek, however, remained dubious. "How are we to know that you are really Bustenai, and not an impostor?" he asked.

"I have no requests to make of you, nor do I demand recognition," replied Bustenai. "On the banks of the rivers Euphrates and Hidekel, there live hundreds of thousands of Jews who know me. Still, if you seek proof now, let your wise and learned men question me. My answers will convince them that I am a pupil of the great Rabbi Chafni, who is my grandfather."

"And what if we believe you?" asked Telek. "What then? What advice can you offer us in our present dilemma?"

"My advice to you, my brothers, is not to forsake our Lord, the G-d of our fathers, and to have faith in Him."

"So you suggest we depart from here, poor and helpless, and wander forth to risk unknown perils?" asked Telek in despairing tones. "We have no idea where we can possibly find a place to rest. How can we look upon the suffering of our poor wives and children?"

"G-d forbid!" answered Bustenai.

"Then I see no alternative between death on the one hand, and accepting Mohammedanism on the other!" said Telek.

"There is another way, my brothers," said Bustenai. "Let us send ambassadors to Mohammed to plead that he allow the Jews to dwell here in peace, as hitherto."

"That will surely be useless," interposed Barak. "Many Jewish communities have already tried that without avail."

"I still think it is worth trying," persisted Bustenai. "Let me accompany your delegation, and perhaps G-d may send His help through me."

The council decided that they had nothing to lose by following Bustenai's suggestion, especially as he seemed so anxious to take part in the delegation. Barak and Telek also agreed to go with him.

Bustenai, whose stay in Arabia had enabled him to observe Mohammed's tactics, knew a great deal about his character, mind, and his relations towards his fellow-men.

On the basis of this knowledge, Bustenai had formed a plan, not only of saving the Jews in Arabia, but those in all other lands where Mohammedanism was disseminated.

Bustenai induced his friend Achai to accompany him. It would be easier for him to carry out his plan if Achai went with him to Medina.

Chapter Twenty-Four

ince Mohammed could neither read nor write, he had to rely upon learned men to assist him. Thus it was that Mohammed's secretary was a Jew by the name of Ibrahim, who was a gifted linguist, a scribe, and a scholar.

And so it was to this Ibrahim that Achai one day presented himself.

"What is your name, and what is the reason for your call?" asked Ibrahim.

"I am Achai, a Persian Jew, a friend of the Jewish prince Bustenai."

"But surely this Bustenai was executed by the Persian Sultan?" said Ibrahim in reply.

"That is where you, like so many others, are mistaken," replied Achai. "It is true that Kuzroi issued a sentence of death against him, but Bustenai is actually still alive. May I ask you something personal?"

"Speak on," answered Ibrahaim.

"I am wondering how you, a Jew, could spend so many years with Mohammed and witness his oppression and persecution of your brethren without doing something about it," remarked Achai boldly.

"Indeed, you misjudge me, sir. Many times have I fallen at the feet of Mohammed and begged him, with tears and pleading, that he cease his cruel persecution of the Jews, but all to no avail. Mohammed is so stubborn and strong-willed that when he makes up his mind to adopt a certain line of action, nothing in the world can alter it!" Ibrahim spoke so earnestly that Acahi had no doubt of the sincerity of his words.

"Then I take it that if there is anything in your power to help the Jews, you would surely be willing to do it?" asked Achai.

"Gladly, and with all my heart," replied Ibrahim.

"Then arrange an interview for me with Mohammed's wife Kafya."

"Stranger, you ask the impossible! I could sooner lead you to the moon than to Mohammed's harem!" cried Ibrahim unhappily.

"Well, can you in some way get a message through to her? I believe she is still a loyal Jewish daughter at heart," said Achai.

"That may be possible," answered Ibrahim slowly.

"Then ask Kafya to tell Mohammed that she had a dream in which King David appeared before her. She must say that King David told her that his grandson would be coming to Medina with a very important message for Mohammed. Ibrahim, I beg of you, if you really want to help your afflicted brethren in their hour of need, get this message through to Kafya. Remember, the fate of hundreds of Jews depends upon your carrying out this mission!"

"Rely upon me to do my best," replied Ibrahim reassuringly.

Kafya was a Jewess who had been the wife of a Hebrew poet named Kinanah. Her husband had died a martyr to the Jewish cause, in Mohammed's "holy wars." When Kafya had been taken captive, together with so many others, Mohammed was enraptured with her beauty and decided to make her his wife. Kafya was powerless to resist and, much against her will, she became his wife. Mohammed treated her with every respect, recognizing that not only was she more beautiful than all his other wives, but that she was also more intelligent. He made her the favorite of his fourteen wives, and she was the queen of the harem. Despite Mohammed's exceptional kindness and generosity towards Kafya, she remained, at heart, true to her Jewish faith and people. Achai therefore felt certain that she would wish to help them now. Surely enough, when Ibrahim's message was brought to her by a trusted servant, Kafya was overjoyed that she had an opportunity of helping her suffering brethren.

The following morning, Kafya decided to go for a ride on her camel. She looked for her footstool with which she usually mounted the beast, but could not see it anywhere. As she was looking around, Mohammed saw her dilemma and came out to her, inclined his head, saying:

"Heavenly Kafya, O daughter of the High Priest Aaron, and niece of the prophet Moses, let me be your footstool and mount over me, to your camel!"

Kafya smiled upon him kindly and said to him: "As you are so good to me, I shall relate a dream I had last night. It was a strange dream, but wonderfully interesting."

"Tell me, fairest flower, what was your dream?"

"Last night in my dream," began Kafya, "a tall, imposing man appeared; his hair was white and his countenance was noble and grave. 'I am King David,' he said, 'and I have a message which you are to convey to Mohammed. Tell him that a grandson of mine is on his way to Mohammed with a very important message for him, and that he will bring him tidings which will prove of benefit to him.' And with that, this old man disappeared."

"Thank you, dear daughter of Israel. May your dream be realized for good!" Kafya gave him a smile and rode off. Mohammed stood there looking after her in admiration.

Chapter Twenty-Five

n that very day, Mohammed had two delegations waiting to see him. One delegation was from a pagan tribe who had come to beg to be allowed to continue worshiping their own god for a period of three more years. When he refused them, they asked for one year or six months more. But Mohammed was adamant. "Either accept my religion, or my warriors will destroy you."

After Mohammed had dismissed the first delegation, he called in the emissaries of the Valley of Vadil-Kara, who had been waiting in the outer court and had heard how the first delegation had been treated.

Bustenai stepped boldly forward and greeted Mohammed:

"Peace, Mohammed! It is indeed well that you are destroying all forms of idol-worship. For this you deserve congratulations. But beware when you persecute those who worship the One and True God!"

"Who are you who dare to address me so boldly!" exclaimed Mohammed.

"I am a grandson of King David!" declared Bustenai.

"Oh yes, I have already been told of your coming by the Angel Gabriel. What message do you bear for me?"

Bustenai saw that Kafya had done her part well. Hardly able to conceal a smile, Bustenai continued:

"Pay heed, Mohammed, to what our Holy Scriptures have written about you! After the destruction of our Holy Temple in Jerusalem, there lived a very wise and holy man. His name was Rabbi Shimon ben Yochai. He was an enemy of the Romans, and they wanted to put him to death. But he escaped, and he hid for thirteen years in a cave, where G-d miraculously provided him with food and water. An angel of G-d appeared to him there and revealed the future to him. That is when he saw you, Mohammed, preaching a new faith to the world. A faith in One G-d Who created the world, the heavens and the earth. That is what our common ancestor, Abraham, preached, too, in olden times. Rabbi Shimon saw you, the descendant of Ishmael, standing with drawn sword, a conqueror of many nations. He saw, too, how your religion and power were spreading throughout the world, and he called out from the depths of his being: 'Have we not suffered enough at the hands of the Romans (of Edom)? Must we now also bleed under the tyrannies of Ishmael?'

"And the Angel of G-d again appeared before him, saying: 'Have no fear, for G-d has given the power to Ishmael only for the purpose of freeing you from the persecution of Edom. G-d will provide them with a leader from their own people, and they will conquer many lands and their power will become so great that a deep hatred will be born between them and the sons of Edom!'

"And now, Mohammed, I know that you are the leader about whom the angel spoke to our Sage, all those hundreds of years ago! Your role is to stamp out all forms of idolatry and spread your teachings throughout many countries. But why must you persecute the Jews, who serve the One and Only G-d! Your mission is to help them, not to treat them as an enemy and seek their destruction!"

"Tell me, stranger, where are these prophecies written of which you speak? And how have they been revealed to you?" asked Mohammed in wonder.

"They are all here," answered Bustenai, tapping a scroll of parchment in his hand. "It is all written down in an old, old script, and this parchment was given to me by my grandfather, the learned Rabbi Chafni."

Mohammed took hold of the scroll of parchment and handed it to his secretary Ibrahim, ordering him to read and translate it.

Ibrahim translated the document into Arabic, whilst Mohammed sat listening attentively. When his secretary had concluded, Mohammed commanded everyone to leave his presence, so that he could speak to Bustenai, alone.

"Tell me, stranger, what is your name?" asked Mohammed.

"I am called Bustenai; my father was Huna, and his father was Mar Chanina, a Jewish prince of the House of David."

"Welcome, Bustenai! And now that we are alone, tell me, is it truly a Divine prophecy that you have brought me?"

"It is certainly so," answered Bustenai.

Mohammed was silent a moment, then addressed Bustenai earnestly: "Bustenai, accept my faith, then all your fellow-Jews will follow your example and will accept Mohammedanism. I will give you my daughter for a wife, and you will inherit all my wealth, as well as my high position."

"Your words have a familiar echo," answered Bustenai. "Another king made a similar offer to me, but just as Kurzroi's offer was made in vain, so is yours. Never will I desert my G-d and His Torah! But Mohammed, listen to me. What need have you of a few impoverished Jews when soon, Egypt, Syria, Greece, Persia, Mesopotamia, Africa and Spain, will all be conquered by you? Leave us in peace to serve our G-d as hitherto! The emissaries who have come from the Jews of the Valley of Vadil-Kara, wait without, for your answer. Make it a favorable one and show that your attitude to those who serve the One G-d is now one of friendship!"

"Very well, Bustenai. I shall grant your request.

But as for you, I ask you to stay here with me in Medina, and act as my counsellor."

With relief and gratitude to the Almighty for His mercies, Telek and Barak brought the joyous tidings to the Jews of Vadil-Kara, who awaited their return with anxious hearts.

Achai meanwhile remained with Bustenai in Medina.

Chapter Twenty-Six

ince Bustenai's coming to Medina, Mohammed's attitude towards the Jews was completely changed. He kept his word, and no Jew suffered religious persecution in Arabia. It is true that Mohammed realized that the number of Jews in the country was so small, that they could hardly be considered any kind of menace to his supremacy. Yet until Bustenai had opened his eyes to this viewpoint, he had not regarded the Jews in such a light.

When Mohammed died, he left no son to succeed him. By right, his son-in-law Ali, was the next in line to succeed him in the caliphate, but Isha, who was the first wife of Mohammed, hated Ali, and prevailed upon the followers of Mohammed to bestow the caliphate upon Mohammed's old friend Abu Beker. And even when, two years later, the latter died, she again prevailed upon the people to bestow the caliphate upon Omer, the brave commander-in-chief of the army. That is how it came about that friction arose among the followers of Mohammed, who were now divided into two camps.

It was about this time that a certain Persian Jew came to Medina on business. He brought greetings to

Bustenai from his mother, Yaleta, and from his grandfather, Rabbi Chafni. Bustenai was overjoyed.

Then the Persian Jew continued more gravely: "We Jews are going through a very hard time in Persia at present. The queen, Artsim-Dakt, is merciless in her ambition to restore Persia to its former glory. Meanwhile, we Jews have to bear the brunt of her ruthlessness. In order to maintain a huge army, she taxes the people without pity, and naturally, she now has a good excuse to extort exorbitant taxes from the Jews, irrespective of their ability to pay such sums."

"This is indeed sad news that you bring," said Bustenai sorrowfully.

"That is not all," continued the visitor. "The queen seems determined to bring idolatry into the country, and has ordered all our Yeshivoth closed. No more can one hear the pleasant voices of our scholars chanting the Talmud at Sura and Pombeditha."

Bustenai's eyes filled with tears. "And," continued the man, "the queen is so heartless that she even abuses her own sister."

"Surely not the gentle Princess Dara!" cried Bustenai.

"Yes, indeed. The queen tried to force her sister to marry the king of the Tartars. When Dara refused, she was imprisoned in a fortress, where even now she pines in solitary confinement."

"Thank you, my friend, though your tidings are truly tragic," said Bustenai.

A wave of homesickness engulfed Bustenai. If only he were back home, perhaps he might find some way of rescuing the unfortunate Princess Dara from her fortress prison. If only he could rescue her now as she had once rescued him!

Bustenai lost no time in calling on the Caliph.

"My lord," said Bustenai to him, "you surely know that Mohammed often followed the advice I gave him."

"Yes, Bustenai, I know it. And if you have any good advice to offer me, I, too, shall be glad to take it," answered the Caliph.

"Then tell me, my lord, why you sit here with folded hands while great deeds and victories await you. You waste your time in petty squabbles when with a little orderly planning you could achieve great things. Look to the south where a great country like Persia is ruled by a spoiled, capricious woman! Get your armies together and conquer these idol-worshippers. I know the country well, for it was my home. Come, and I shall lead your armies there to conquer it!"

The Caliph was very pleased with Bustenai's suggestion, and he quickly summoned his armies to march against Persia. At the head of the army rode Saed, the commander in-chief, with whom Bustenai was very friendly. Bustenai and Achai accompanied this Arab army, full of hope and optimism.

Bustenai was riding beside Saed when the latter suddenly asked him:

"How old are you, Bustenai? And how is it that you have never married?"

"Oh, my friend, before I can think of myself and my personal happiness, I have a very important task to fulfill. In Persia, there is a very dear friend of mine, who is suffering imprisonment. She is the Princess Dara, daughter of the late King Kuzroi. Before all else, I must find some way of freeing her, or I cannot find peace of mind." And Bustenai proceeded to tell Saed all that Dara had done for him while he lived at the palace.

Meanwhile, the Persian court at Ktesipon was a hotbed of terror and intrigue. When Artsim-Dakt heard of the approaching Arab armies, she announced that she herself would go out to meet them at the head of her soldiers. She appointed Harmuz, an old friend of her father's, commander-in-chief. This aroused the envy of a rival field-marshal named Rustem. With the aid of a treacherous noble of the court, Yesdegerd, Rustem put Artsim-Dakt to death. Rustem then proclaimed Yesdegerd king of Persia.

Yesdegerd remained at the palace while Rustem went forth at the head of the Persian army to defend the country.

The ebb and flow of the battle brought victories to both sides. Sometimes the tide of battle favored the Arabs, sometimes the Persians. Finally, after a march upon the Persian capital, victory was in the hands of the Arabs.

Yesdegerd saw no alternative but to capitulate and sue for peace with Saed.

Saed sent back the following ultimatum: "Accept our faith! We give you our word that no Arab will ever set foot upon your soil, except for the purpose of collecting the dues that all followers of Mohammed gladly pay. If you refuse to accept our faith, you will be compelled to pay a ransom, the sum of which we shall name. Should you fail to accept either of these two propositions, your only course is to meet us on the battlefield and settle the matter there!"

Yesdegerd was so infuriated at the degrading propositions sent him by Saed, that he ordered sacks of earth be tied around the necks of Saed's messengers and that they be sent back thus to their Arab leader!

In the meantime, Bustenai and Achai departed for Mechuza. It was eight long years since Bustenai had seen his beloved mother and grandfather. The longing, the joy, the tears, and the embraces of that reunion were indescribable. Precious as their meeting was, Bustenai had to tear himself away. It was war, and there was a great battle to be won before he could return in peace to his dear ones.

Bustenai hoped that, with G-d's help, the Persian armies, greater in number though they were, would be beaten. Then the Jews would be able to live in freedom from persecution and in peace with their neighbors. Bustenai went out among his fellow Jews and exhorted them to rally under his flag, so that they, together with the Arabs, could go forth and conquer the idolatrous Persians.

The Jews needed no urging; they rallied to Bustenai's call and lost no time in marching along the banks of the River Euphrates, upstream towards the spot where the Persian and Arab armies were facing each other.

Before Bustenai's arrival, the two armies had engaged in heated and bloody battle, without either side having won a decisive victory.

The Persian commander-in-chief of the armies, Rustem, had taken his vast army across the Euphrates, confident that he would quickly overpower the smaller Arab forces. But when the two armies hurled themselves at each other, at a place called Kadessia, the battles raged for three days, sometimes favoring one side, sometimes the other.

At the end of the third day, both sides were beginning to weary. Bustenai appeared on the battlefront with his eager, fresh Jewish troops, who hurled themselves heroically at the Persian forces and broke through their defenses on all sides.

The battle raged furiously all night, and at dawn, the Persian leader, Rustem, fell. When the Persians saw that their commander-in-chief was slain, they fled from the battlefield in disarray.

Chapter Twenty-Seven

ing Yesdegerd had not a moment's doubt that the brave Rustem, with the vastly superior Persian forces, would not overwhelm the weak Arab army. His main concern was his own position as king of Persia. Had not his three predecessors been killed, one after the other? He wanted to make certain that his court would not get embroiled in the intrigue that could end his reign and life.

After pondering the matter deeply, he came to the conclusion that the best way of safeguarding his position would be to marry Princess Dara, the daughter of the royal Persian cout, the last member of the holy House of Sassan.

Yesdegerd gave the orders that Princess Dara be taken out of her fortress-prison and brought to him immediately.

Yesdegerd received her in a most friendly fashion.

"Princess Dara, I regret that your sister saw fit to keep you imprisoned for so long. I am happy to give you your freedom. In fact, it is my wish and desire to set you on the Persian throne, where you rightly belong."

"Are you not the one who murdered my sister?" was Dara's rejoinder.

"Have you forgotten that your sister was your enemy?" Yesdegerd reminded her. "I, on the other hand, intend to be your friend!"

"If you are trying to suggest that I become your wife, you are just wasting your time. I would never marry the murderer of my father's daughter!" cried Princess Dara.

Yesdegerd had difficulty in controlling his temper, but he was determined to gain his end by gentle means if at all possible.

"Listen, dear princess. Be reasonable. I simply must marry you to strengthen my position on the throne. Why not cooperate with me and be my friend. It will be to our mutual advantage and ensure peace at the court and throughout the land!"

"I have already told you that nothing will make me change my mind. Nothing would ever make me agree to become the wife of my sister's murderer," Dara repeated obstinately.

When Yesdegerd saw that his gentle remonstration was yielding no results, he became white with fury and disappointment.

"You ungrateful girl! I offer you the Persian throne if you will become my wife, and you throw my offer back in my teeth! You shall die, Princess Dara. Will that please you better?"

"Death will be infinitely sweeter to me, than life

with you, foul murderer!" replied Dara fearlessly.

At this very moment, the door of the king's chamber flung open. In rushed several bedraggled blood-besmirched soldiers, crying as they rushed in:

"Your Majesty! Quickly, quickly, make your escape! Woe unto us! Your armies are vanquished! Rustem is dead! The Jews and Arabs are coming! Hurry, Your Majesty, they may be here any moment!"

Yesdegerd could hardly believe his own ears! Forgotten was the Princess, forgotten the Persian throne. All he now thought of was how best to save his own skin. There was great wealth at the palace, but Yesdegerd barely had time to gather some jewels, pearls, diamonds, and a few personal items of clothing and run, he was not yet sure whither!

Yesdegerd had taken precious jewels and only regretted that he could take no more. Little did he know that they were to prove his undoing. When he and his few trusted followers reached an inn where they planned to spend the night, the innkeeper recognized his royal guests. He learned that they had brought valuables with them, and the temptation proved too much for him. In the depth of the night he set upon his sleeping guests, killed them all, and threw their bodies into the nearby river. The swift-flowing stream carried them along in the darkness, right into the sea, and no one knew what had become of them.

Chapter Twenty-Eight

Great was the jubilation in the hearts of the Jews throughout Persia as Bustenai marched through with his victorious Jewish army. Bustenai made his way to Mechuza, where his beloved mother, Yaleta, and his dear grandfather, Rabbi Chafni, awaited him with yearning, their hearts overflowing with joy and gratitude for Bustenai's safe and triumphant return.

Achai at long last was reunited with his beloved bride, from whom he had been torn under the wedding canopy!

Saed, the conqueror, the whole of Persia in his hands, insisted that the Persians give up their idolatry and embrace Mohammedanism. The Jews, on the other hand, were granted complete religious freedom by the Caliph, who sent a special messenger to Bustenai, informing him that he was appointed "Resh-Galuta" (Prince-in-Exile) of the Jews.

The Yeshivot of Sura and Pombeditha again threw open their doors, and students from far and near flocked to study Torah. Once again the halls resounded with the melodious chanting of the Talmud; once again hundreds gathered to listen to Rabbi Chafni's brilliant "shiurim" (lectures).

Bustenai appointed his friend, the learned Achai, to be "Rosh Yeshivha" in Nehardea, where Bustenai had reopened the Yeshivah.* Achai soon became famous for his great knowledge, and he is known to this day for his great work "Sheiltoth."

When Saed came to Ktesipon, he learned that the Princess Dara was held captive there. He immediately commanded that the princess be treated with perfect courtesy and honor as befitted one of royal birth. He continued on his mission of ensuring that all Persia, without exception, accepted the Mohammedan religion.

First, Saed went north, where he had some "mopping up" to do of remnants of the Persian army. When he reached the province of Shushan, where the Satrap (Governor) Harmozan was in power. Saed seized Harmozan and condemned him to death.

When Harmozan was brought before him, he begged Saed to allow him to have a drink of water before he was killed. Saed granted this final request. Harmozan was still not satisfied and observed to Saed: "I am afraid that someone may kill me whilst I am drinking." To which Saed replied: "You have my word that you will not be put to death until you have drunk the water in this goblet."

On hearing this, the quick-witted Harmozan im-

---

*The yeshivah in Nehardea was originally founded by Samuel, contemporary of Rav.

mediately hurled the goblet away, spilling the water onto the ground.

"I have your word, Saed, that I am not to be killed until I drink this water. That is now impossible, for as you see, it has already seeped into the ground at our feet."

Harmozan was allowed to live on condition that he, too, accept Mohammedanism. This he did, and all his fellow Satraps followed his example.

Before leading his conquering armies into Egypt, Saed paid a visit to his friend Bustenai in Mechuza. Saed greeted Bustenai with affection and joyfully told him of the astounding Arabian victories. Surely Bustenai, who had fought so valiantly side by side with the Arabs, and who had won so many battles for them, deserved to share the spoils. When Bustenai adamantly refused to accept anything, Saed remonstrated with him over the injustice of his refusal.

"You must accept my offer in fairness to your fellow Jews who were so heavily taxed under Persian rule. Now you have an opportunity of recompensing them, in part, for their losses. And for you, too, my friend, I have brought a special gift." At a sign from Saed, a heavily veiled woman was led slowly into the room.

"This woman is a captive," said Saed, "and I have brought her to be your slave. Take her; she is yours."

At these words, the woman lifted her veil from her face. Bustenai cried out in surprise and delight: "Dara! 'tis you!" "I am happy and honored to be your slave," she said in a low voice. Bustenai's eyes filled with tears. "What are you saying, Princess Dara? Have you forgotten that I owe my life to you. Arise, Dara; long live Dara the Queen!"

* After Dara truthfully converted to Judaism according to Halacha, she and Bustenai were married.

Chapter Twenty-Nine

ustenai was the forerunner of a line of princes that were the leaders of Israel, until a tyrannical Caliph abolished the institution of "Resh Galuta," thereby depriving the Jews of political independence.

* * *

Many hundreds of years have passed since Bustenai lived. No longer does the House of David rule in Israel. But the flames of faith and courage that King David kindled, and that Bustenai staunchly guarded, will burn brightly in the heart of every Jew, until the coming of our righteous redeemer, the descendant of David.